Monika Wegler

Dwarf Rabbits

Everything about Purchase, Diet, and Care
to Keep Rabbits Healthy

With Color Photos by the Author
and Drawings by Fritz W. Köhler

Consulting Editor: Lucia Vriends-Parent

New York/London/Toronto/Sydney

The color photos on the covers show:
Front cover: Red dwarf rabbits (female with her five-week-old young).
Inside front cover: Siamese dwarf rabbit (female).
Inside back cover: Lop-eared Thuringian dwarf rabbit (male, ten weeks old).
Back cover: Above left: Thuringian dwarf rabbit, twenty days old. Above right: Black-and-tan dwarf rabbit, five weeks old. Below (from left to right): Havanna, Lop-eared Squirrel Gray, and White-tipped Black dwarf rabbits.

First English language edition published in 1986 by Barron's Educational Series, Inc.
© 1985 by Gräfe und Unzer GmbH, Munich
Translated from the German by Rita and Robert Kimber.
The title of the German edition is *Zwergkaninchen*.

Second edition - Munich: Gräfe und Unzer, 1986
Second edition 1986
Production: Robert Gigler

All inquiries should be addressed to:
Barron's Educational Series, Inc.
250 Wireless Boulevard
Hauppauge, New York 11788

International Standard Book No. 0-8120-3669-7
Library of Congress Catalog Card No. 86-1121

Library of Congress Cataloging-in-Publication Data
Wegler, Monika.
    Dwarf rabbits.

    Translation of: Zwergkaninchen.
    Includes index.
    1. Dwarf rabbits.   I. Title.
SF455.D85W4413   1986   636'.9322   86-1121
ISBN 0-8120-3669-7

Printed in Hong Kong
  0   490   9 8 7

About the Author

Monika Wegler is a professional photographer and journalist as well as the mother of two children. Her household includes a dwarf rabbit for each member of the family. Ms. Wegler has published numerous articles and photo series in various magazines. Her special interest is photographing animals and children. All the color photos in this pet owner's guide were taken by her especially for this volume.

Advice and Warning

This book deals with the keeping and care of dwarf rabbits as pets. In working with these animals, you may occasionally sustain minor scratches or bites. Have such wounds treated by a doctor at once.

As a result of unhygienic living conditions, rabbits can have mites and other external parasites, some of which can be transmitted to humans or to pet animals, including cats and dogs. Have the infested rabbit treated by a veterinarian at once (see page 34), and go to the doctor yourself at the slightest suspicion that you may be harboring one of these pests. When buying a rabbit, be sure to look for the signs of parasite infestation.

Rabbits must be watched very carefully during the necessary and regular exercise period in the house (see pages 21–22). To avoid life-threatening accidents, be particularly careful that your pet does not gnaw on any electrical wires.

Contents

Preface

Our household includes not only two children and a cat but also three cute dwarf rabbits. When my two children play with Mohrle, Trixi, and Mümmi—the names of the rabbits—our cat, Naughty, makes for a quiet corner on a shelf. Two lively children and three rabbits darting all over the apartment are too much for him, playful as he is. At first I always made a point to be around during play sessions or when the children petted their rabbits, explaining patiently again and again that rabbits have their own special needs and ways. I insisted that the children be aware of this when handling the animals, and that they respect the peculiarities of their playmates. For I have noticed repeatedly that not only children but adults as well assume that a dwarf rabbit will always be as sweet and gentle as it looks. Then it comes as a great shock, especially for children, if the cute little bunny scratches or—worse yet—bites. Are dwarf rabbits mean creatures? Not at all.

Dwarf rabbits quickly become tame and friendly, and they are very fond of being petted if they are treated properly and their natural patterns of behavior are accepted (see Understanding Dwarf Rabbits, page 51). Drawing on years of experience with dwarf rabbits, I describe in some detail how to treat dwarf rabbits. Parents will be interested in my suggestions on teaching children to appreciate these lovable pets and assisting children until they can look after their rabbits pretty much on their own. In our family it took quite a while before both children were able to assume full responsibility for their dwarf rabbits. An occasional helping hand or some advice is necessary even later to prevent mistakes.

Dwarf rabbits are quite often kept or fed improperly. A one-sided diet, or one that does not reflect these animals' nutritional needs, as well as a lack of exercise results in obesity and heart disease, which may lead to premature death. This pet owner's guide contains many suggestions for proper feeding. Proper housing and the treatment of sicknesses and injuries are also discussed, and some space is devoted to breeding, which is not always a simple matter in the case of miniature breeds. In a special chapter, the main dwarf breeds and color varieties currently bred in the United States and Great Britain are described, and the text is supplemented by color photos, all of which are published here for the first time.

Unlike cats and dogs, rabbits are almost entirely silent. They don't yowl, bark, or meow, and the expressions of pleasure or pain are largely limited to body language. That is why I have devoted considerable space to the body language of dwarf rabbits. Knowing this language will help you recognize, for instance, whether your rabbit is in a mood to be petted or would rather rest. The better you can interpret the behavior and needs of your dwarf rabbit, the easier it will be to treat the animal properly, and the more pleasure you will derive from having a healthy and spirited companion.

This pet owner's guide incorporates not only the owner's personal experience but also the knowledge and advice of many rabbit breeders and other experts. I should like to express here my special thanks to Mr. Josef Singer, State Breed Judge for Upper Bavaria (West Germany), for checking the manuscript; and to Dr. Gabriele Wiesner, veterinarian, for her assistance in preparing the chapter Health Care and Diseases. I should also like to thank Fritz W. Köhler for his excellent drawings.

Considerations Before You Buy

Is a Dwarf Rabbit the Right Pet for You?

There is hardly a creature that looks more like a toy than a dwarf rabbit. The round button eyes, the relatively large head on the small body, the rounded cheeks, and the soft fur make this animal almost irresistible. But remember that dwarf rabbits can live five years—and up to ten years in some cases—if well cared for. That is a long time. So if you find yourself in a pet store holding a cute bunny in your arms, pause a few minutes and run through the following questions to make sure a dwarf rabbit is indeed the pet you want.

• If you have a family, does everyone in the household share your desire for a pet rabbit?
• If you have no yard or balcony, do you have at least one room in your apartment where no one smokes, where the radio or TV is not on constantly, and where there are no treasured rugs or expensive pieces of furniture to worry about? (See page 16.)
• A dwarf rabbit has to have a chance to run outside its cage regularly. If your pet bunny should not take to house training (see page 20), will you resent cleaning up rabbit droppings?
• Do you leave home on vacations? If you don't want to take your pet along on a trip and don't know anyone who can take care of him while you're gone, you'll have to pay to board him.
• Will you have time in your busy life to devote *at least* one hour a day to your rabbit?
• If your rabbit should get sick, will you give up a weekend trip to stay home and attend to him? And if necessary, will you take him to the veterinarian, knowing the fee

might be considerable, perhaps exceeding the original price you paid for him?

If you have answered every question with an unhesitating yes, no dwarf rabbit could

Dwarf rabbits are neat and clean by nature. They wash themselves all over, including the feet, every day.

wish for a better owner. If, however, you responded with one or more no's, reconsider the matter. Perhaps with some further thought, you will discover a different kind of pet to suit your circumstances better.

Is a Pair Happier than a Single Rabbit?

A single pet rabbit can be kept happy if you are able to spend a little time with it several times during the day. In other words, it is not enough to feed the animal and take care of its basic needs. You also have to pet your rabbit and lavish some attention on him. If, in addition to this, you can provide him with some change and excitement, and can let him run free some of the time, his spirits will remain high and he won't grow apathetic.

If circumstances won't permit this, you should buy two female baby rabbits from the same litter. Two animals that have grown up together usually get along well. Don't try to do your doe (female rabbit) a favor by getting her an unrelated companion of the same sex. The two animals would get into serious fights. Older animals pummel newly introduced ones, even if the newcomers are only seven weeks old. In a large enough run, female rabbits that don't get along will avoid each other; that is, the weaker one will respect the more powerful one without challenging her. In the case of male rabbits (called bucks), however, contests over rank are bound to occur, and can cause serious injuries. It is therefore not advisable to keep two bucks together. Remember in all this that fights are not a sign of ''badness'' on your rabbits' part. Rabbits are not humans. Their behavior is in keeping with their nature, and it does not follow human rules.

There remains one other alternative, and that is to buy a true pair. But think twice before you take this step. Chances are the two animals will indeed get along famously, but unless you have the buck neutered (see right), you will have to find some way of housing the offspring. If you don't plan to raise rabbits commercially but simply would like to watch a litter or two grow up, you'd do better to borrow a buck later on to father some babies.

Male or Female?

Any dwarf rabbit, whether male or female, can become a tame and affectionate pet or can remain shy and fearful. It depends almost entirely on whether or not you treat the animal properly. But if you have a male rabbit and plan to keep him indoors most of

the time, have him neutered. This minor operation not only renders the animal incapable of reproducing, but—if performed early enough, preferably when the rabbit is about four months old—also largely prevents spraying later on. (Male rabbits mark their territory and their mates with urine; see page 54.) The operation also tones down their overall behavior, so that afterwards a male and female dwarf rabbit can be kept together without problems. But castrated rabbits do tend to obesity, and it is important that you plan an especially well-balanced diet (see page 25) for a neutered male.

How to Sex a Rabbit

Sexing a young rabbit is not a simple matter and requires some experience. Many a customer has left a pet store thinking he had two female siblings and found later on that he had a mixed pair. If you have any doubt about your rabbit's sex you can have a commercial breeder have a look at it. But why don't you try to sex the rabbit yourself first? Place the animal in your lap facing away from you. Slide one hand under it and tilt it backward until you can see the belly. If you don't lay the rabbit flat on its back but lean it against you, the animal will be more likely to cooperate. Now spread the fur between the back legs gently, and you'll see two small, roundish raised spots: the anus and the sexual orifice (see drawing on page 7). At first glance both openings seem round, but if you stretch the skin around the sexual orifice a little by pressing down very gently with your middle and index fingers, the penis—if the rabbit is male—will protrude. In males the sexual orifice is always round, and there is a space between it and the anus. Females have a small slitlike organ

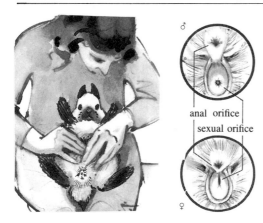

anal orifice

sexual orifice

Determining the sex: If you place the rabbit on your lap as shown, you can see the sexual and anal orifices. (The enlarged detail at the top shows a male; the one below, a female.)

that looks like a fine line running toward the anus. The vaginal opening and the anus are practically next to each other.

Children and Dwarf Rabbits

Dwarf rabbits are often bought as presents for children. But I would not advise giving a rabbit to a child under five years. It is hard for children this young to learn how to get hold of a struggling rabbit and pick it up properly. The animal may become frightened and respond by scratching or biting. If it is dropped, it may get hurt. Meanwhile your child will come running up to you, upset and in tears because "the bunny was so mean." Very small children also find it harder to relate to a rather "incommunica-tive" rabbit than to a kitten that mews or a dog that barks. It is not uncommon for misunderstandings to arise that leave both the animal and the child unhappy. Older children, however, can derive much enjoy-

ment and can learn many useful lessons from having pet rabbits around. But even older children need some assistance and an occasional explanation from adults in looking after their pets.

Being the mother in a household with two school-age children, three dwarf rabbits, and a cat, I have some pertinent experience, and I should like to give you a few tips that may help avoid some typical crises in everyday family life with pets. First, define clearly who is in charge of which animal and who does which jobs. Teach yourself to stick to your own rules, and then insist that everybody else do his or her part; otherwise you'll end up doing all the chores yourself. In our household pet care continued to be a source of conflict until my children and I sat down together to draw up a weekly schedule of chores. To make the project a little more fun, everyone got to choose a color with which to mark the tasks he or she was responsible for on the different days of the week. The chores to be done are: feeding, cleaning the cage, removing the droppings, collecting dandelion greens, and taking the rabbit outdoors. If you include yourself in the work crew, the children are less likely to feel overworked when schoolwork begins to take up more of their time. Having pets continues to be fun, and—most important of all—the children learn to take responsibility for other creatures.

Dwarf Rabbits and Other Household Pets

As a rule, dwarf rabbits and guinea pigs get along well and can sometimes even be kept together in a large cage. Cats and dogs don't adjust so quickly to a new rabbit. Because of their hunting instinct they may regard the newcomer as potential prey. The chances for peaceful coexistence are best if these different animals grow up together. But older animals, too, can learn to live together and respect each other.

When introducing a dwarf rabbit, observe the following rules:

• Never neglect the old-timers and their rights because of the new pet.
• Let the dwarf rabbit get accustomed to its new life before you introduce it to the other pets. Never leave unsupervised two animals that are just getting acquainted. Make sure the rabbit stays in its cage; if you let it out you're asking for trouble. Don't rush anything; pet both animals and talk to them in a kind and soothing voice. If the dog starts to bark or the cat tries to swat the rabbit, scold the offender firmly and briefly.
• If you think that the animals have gotten used to each other, let the rabbit out of the cage for its first free run. But be sure to stay nearby. Only close observation and experience will show if or when you can leave the two animals together without supervision.

Some animals belonging to different species develop amazing friendships, but in other cases all efforts to foster mutual tolerance are in vain. If this is the case you simply have to accept that fact and keep the two pets away from each other.

There are no general rules that always hold, for every dog and cat is different. I also have found that dwarf rabbits vary greatly in their reaction to other animals. Naughty, our male cat, came to live with us as a ten-week-old kitten. We already had our three dwarf rabbits at the time. Naughty was a very playful and temperamental kitten and tried to play with the rabbits as

soon as he had a chance, pummeling them with his feet the way kittens and cats do. Mohrle, our youngest dwarf rabbit, would have none of this nonsense and made herself scarce. She avoids Naughty to this day, even though the cat never really hurt her. Trixi, our second-oldest rabbit, is playful and extremely nosy. She would sometimes join in the cat's play, executing the most daring leaps, but she always knew how to let the cat know when he was playing too rough. Mümmi, the boss—a Thuringian dwarf rabbit—reacted in a completely different manner from the other two. She refused to put up with any sort of rival, and cuffed the cat so vigorously whenever he dared approach her that to this day he runs off or jumps onto a high shelf when Mümmi comes charging unexpectedly around a corner. The two chase each other and live in perpetual jealousy.

When it's time to clean house I generally let the rabbits have free run of the apartment before I start cleaning. Mümmi always takes advantage of the opportunity to hop to the cat's food dish as quickly as she can. If there is any milk left in it she laps it up with great relish. The cat, filled with resentment, sits on a chair but does not dare descend. But one day he decided to have his revenge. After Mümmi had "desecrated" his dish, he ran to the rabbit's cage and proceeded to eat her grain, making a face like a child who is forced to swallow cod-liver oil. It

Purebred dwarf rabbits and mongrels.
Above left: Two Black-and-Tan dwarf rabbits about six weeks old. Above right: Typical dwarf rabbit mongrels about ten weeks old. Below: A typical dwarf cross on the left and a purebred White-tipped Black dwarf on the right; both about six weeks old. The differences in size and body type are apparent.

was perfectly clear that he detested the taste of the stuff, but he was determined to finish it. That was the first and only time I saw a cat eat grain.

Vacation Care

You can leave your rabbit alone for a day without worry as long as you provide enough food and water. But make sure the cage is not exposed to the direct sun, or your dwarf rabbit might suffer sunstroke. Rabbits prefer to spend hot summer days in the shade.

Are you one of those people who are so busy getting ready for a trip that they forget some of the most important things? Then suddenly somebody asks, "What about our. . .?" But by that time it's too late to find a good solution. Please don't let this happen. Think ahead and ask yourself who will look after your rabbit while you're gone, unless you plan to take him along on the trip.

The following are some of the possibilities:

• You may be able to board your rabbit at the pet store where you bought him.
• A friend who is knowledgeable about rabbits may take your pet or look after it at your house.
• Someone may adopt your rabbit temporarily. Many organizations interested in the welfare of animals keep lists of people who are willing to take in pets for short periods in exchange for a small fee.

Prize-winning bucks.
Above left: Dwarf Squirrel Gray. Above right: White-tipped Black dwarf. Center left: Siamese dwarf. Center right: Havanna dwarf. Below left: Lop-eared Thuringian dwarf. Below right: Lop-eared Chinchilla dwarf.

• You can take your rabbit to a place that boards pets, but be sure to visit and examine the establishment beforehand because not all of them are well run.

Traveling with a Dwarf Rabbit
If you are one of those lucky people with a vacation home in the country—an old farm, a simple cabin, or whatever—take your rabbit along on your vacation. You'll have room for the cage, and you'll probably have more time for your pet than usual, which will make this a special time for your rabbit as well. However, I would not recommend taking a rabbit along on trips to hot, southern regions. Even though rabbits have a thinner coat in summer, they suffer from high heat.

If you take a long trip by car, don't drive for hours without stopping. Take a break every couple of hours. If you stop to eat or drink something, remember your rabbit, too. Letting him hop around a bit on a leash— but not right next to the highway—is as important to him as stretching your legs is to you. Let the rabbit travel in a special transport box that is large enough for him to stretch out but not so large that he slides around in it. Don't put the box next to the motor or in full sun, and, above all, don't put it in the trunk. Many a pet has suffocated in the trunk of a car because there was not enough air.

If you take a trip abroad, find out ahead of time about regulations governing the entry of animals into the country or countries you wish to visit. Some countries—in Europe, for instance—require nothing more than an official health certificate issued by a veterinarian. For other countries, inquire in good time at the appropriate customs office what immunizations or other health records are required.

Advice for Buying a Dwarf Rabbit

Just What Is a Dwarf Rabbit?

The term dwarf rabbit is sometimes used rather loosely by pet dealers and in newspaper ads, and the animals offered for sale under that label frequently turn out to be crosses between dwarf and regular rabbits. What was supposed to be a dwarf rabbit then grows to a weight of five or seven pounds, at which point it may no longer fit into the cage bought for it. Such an animal is likely to end up at an animal shelter or be turned over to the local rabbit breeders' club. I certainly don't mean to suggest that the trade in pet rabbits be restricted to expensive purebreds. A cross that has non-standard coloration—as long as it stays small—will give you as much pleasure as a fancy purebred. But you shouldn't have to end up with a chunky meat animal if a dainty dwarf rabbit is what you wanted.

The Difference between a Purebred Animal and a Mongrel

Pictures are the easiest way to show you how to recognize whether a baby bunny is a true dwarf or not. Look at the bottom color photo on page 9. You will see some clear differences between the two rabbits depicted. Both animals are six weeks old; the one on the left is a cross; the one at the right, a purebred dwarf. The drawing on the right makes the same point. Dwarf rabbits are not simply normal rabbits bred for smaller size. The animals' proportions are different in the two classes of breeds. In the course of time, dwarfs have become more gnomelike. The head is disproportionately large and massive. The skull is broad with a strongly rounded forehead. The neck is barely visible, so that it looks as though the head were attached directly to the body. These traits

are absent in mongrels, as the color photo demonstrates. The head of the rabbit on the left is smaller in relation to the body and not as massive, and the neck is more evident. The entire shape of this rabbit is more elongated.

Offspring of dwarf and normal-sized parents, shown for comparison with a purebred dwarf. The most obvious characteristics of a purebred dwarf (below) are its bold, disproportionately large head, the short ears, and the "cobby" body. These traits are almost totally absent in the cross above.

A true dwarf rabbit is supposed to be compactly built, with a squat, "cobby" body and a short back line. His eyes are big, bright, and slightly protruding, as round as possible, with clearly arched bones over them. The ears are another distinguishing feature; they are short (not more than two inches), set close together, and carried erect. They should be rounded at the tips and well furred; any crossing (called scissor-eared) is a serious fault. If you compare the two six-week-old bunnies in the photo, you'll notice right away that the mongrel has longer ears than the purebred dwarf. So if you want to be sure that the rabbit you are about to buy is really a dwarf, watch for the typical features I've just described. A purebred animal is always the result of controlled breeding, for which specific guidelines are set up (see page 39). Crosses are the result of spontaneous matings or of propagation initiated by humans. Let me illustrate the difference by referring to dogs. Everyone knows what poodles, dachshunds, or German shepherd dogs are. They are different breeds of dogs. If dogs of different breeds mate, the offspring are mongrels that may exhibit traits of all the breeds in their genetic background. Nobody has checked or kept a record of the dogs' ancestors. The situation is the same for cats—and for dwarf rabbits.

Dwarf rabbits that are not purebreds come in all shades of often very pretty colors. Don't be disappointed if your rabbit differs in some respects from the breed standard. If you're not set on breeding rabbits, a pet bunny of mixed background can give you just as much pleasure as a purebred dwarf. But if you want some assurance that your rabbit will stay small, choose a young rabbit that resembles a true dwarf as much as possible. To help you with this, here is a list of typical features of purebred dwarf rabbits. Consult it when you buy a dwarf rabbit.

What a Purebred Dwarf Rabbit Should Look Like

A purebred dwarf rabbit is supposed to display certain traits that are defined in the breed standard. (This standard is drawn up by the Standard Committee of an official rabbit breeders' association—in the United States, by the American Netherland Dwarf Rabbit Club [ANDRC]). At exhibitions the rabbits are judged as to how closely they conform to this standard of perfection. The following guidelines apply to all dwarf breeds except for lop-eared dwarf rabbits.

Weight: At least 1½ lb. (.7 kg); ideally 2½ to 2¾ lb. (1.15–1.25 kg); maximum 3 lb. 5 oz. (1.5 kg).

Shape and build: Squat, cylindrical body that is equally broad at the front and the back; short back line, well rounded hindquarters. Head large in relation to the body, with wide forehead and broad muzzle. The forehead should measure ca. 2¼ inches (5.5 cm) across in a buck and 2 inches (5 cm) in a doe. No visible narrowing between the head and the body. Eyes are large and "bold" or protruding.

Ears: The ears should be in keeping with overall dwarf size. They should be set close together, have rounded tips, and be well furred.

Length of ears: 1¾ to 2¼ inches (4.5–5.5 cm). Ears longer than 2¾ inches (7 cm) are not permitted.

Fur: The fur is judged for quality and length.

Special breed characteristics: Different colors and markings (see page 45).

Where You Can Buy Dwarf Rabbits

Purebred dwarf rabbits are sold at reputable pet stores and they can, of course, be obtained from breeders. Breeders often sell baby rabbits with minor flaws (such as claws of the wrong color or ears that are too long) at a lower price. You can get addresses of breeders from rabbit breeders' clubs (see Useful Addresses, page 55).

It is a pity that most people, when they decide to get a rabbit, think only in terms of a cute little baby bunny, and never consider the possibility of taking in an older animal. Yet it is the older rabbits that end up in animal shelters—rabbits that have lost their charming baby look, may have some bad habits, or are simply old, perhaps infirm, and have therefore been abandoned at a parking lot next to a trash can. I certainly don't mean to spoil your enjoyment of a baby bunny, let alone talk you out of buying one; I only want to remind you that there are homeless older rabbits, some of which may be potentially just as affectionate and lovable as younger ones. Perhaps you are an inveterate animal lover with a large garden, where there would be room for an extra rabbit. If you have the space, why not consider taking a creature at a shelter?

What to Watch for When Buying a Rabbit

You are probably looking forward to many years of companionship with your rabbit. It is all the more important, then, that you take time to choose the right animal. Have a good look at the rabbits that are available and don't fall for the first one with a cute black spot on his nose or the first pair of irresistible dark button eyes. Remember how annoying and emotionally upsetting it will be if you have to keep taking your pet to the veterinarian's or if your rabbit dies prematurely. Here are a few tips.

• A healthy rabbit, especially a young one, is active and curious. If you slowly reach your hand out toward it, it will come hopping up to it. If it stays sitting in a corner without showing any interest in its surroundings, it may be sick. It is possible, of course, that the animal is simply tired and wants to sleep. In the table on page 35 there are some signs that will help you recognize whether a rabbit is healthy or sick.

• If a dwarf rabbit responds to your cautious overtures by hopping away in a panic, you

had better not buy it. Some dwarf rabbits are excessively timid from the time they are very young. These are often animals that were raised in dark hutches or come from breeders who are intent only on production

Attack posture: The tensed body, extended neck, and upward pointing tail mean "Watch out!"

without any interest in the animals as such, or the behavior may be inherited. I have met a number of such timid rabbits, and I had one myself for a long time. It never became really tame even though we treated it with patience and love. Later on, timid baby rabbits such as this may turn into biters (they bite out of fear), or they may be so nervous that they run head-on into furniture when something startles them. These things happen, and they are not necessarily to be attributed to a keeper's mismanagement.

The Age of Your New Rabbit
Dwarf rabbits are often sold at six weeks, but in the case of somewhat delicate animals, it is better to leave them with their mother a little longer. If you wait until your rabbit is eight to ten weeks old it will be big enough to fare well on its own.

Some pet dealers offer tiny rabbits for sale that were separated from their mothers much too early. That is why it's better to shop only at reputable pet stores or buy directly from a breeder.

Housing and Equipment

The Right Indoor Cage

The pet trade offers many cages designed to house small animals like rabbits. These cages are easy to clean and usually quite durable, and perfect for people living in apartments. They all have a plastic tray on the bottom, but the design and material of the cage on top varies. You can choose between a removable cage top of wire grating (see drawing right) or one of plastic. Plastic cages have a section made out of wire grating, which allows you to take the animal out and which also regulates air flow. For dwarf rabbits, wire cages are best. Though the plastic cages offer good protection against drafts and keep the litter from being kicked out of the cage I don't like them because these "plastic homes for animals" remind me of miniature greenhouses.

In heated rooms or if the sun shines in, heat can build up in a plastic cage. The relatively small opening at the top often is not enough to lower the temperature significantly, and excessive heat can quickly lead to death (see Heat Stroke, page 33). Also, the plastic walls isolate the animal by cutting down on its contact with the environment through its finely tuned senses of hearing and smell. That is why I strongly recommend that you buy a wire cage, which is so much airier. When choosing the cage, make sure the plastic tray at the bottom measures at least 18 by 28 inches (45 x 70 cm) and has sides at least 5½ inches (14 cm) high. If the tray is shallower, the litter or bedding will fly all over the room when the rabbit scratches in it. Some cages have a total height of 16 inches (40 cm); others are only 12 inches (30 cm) high. This smaller size will do, but if you want to set up a little box or house for your rabbit inside the cage, a height of 16 inches is better, because it allows your dwarf rabbit to lie on the flat roof of his house comfortably underneath the wire top of the cage. Also check to make sure the plastic tray at the bottom is sturdy.

Some wire cages open from the top; others have doors on the sides through which the rabbit can hop. The cages with tops that flip open make it easier to reach in and take the rabbit out, whereas those with openings on the sides have the advantage that the rabbit can come and go as it pleases.

A cage suitable for a dwarf rabbit kept indoors. The top flips up, making it easier to feed the rabbit and take it out.

The Proper Location

If your rabbit is going to spend most of his time indoors, where you place his cage is very important. When you choose the spot, consider the following points:

• Never place the cage near a window in such a way that it is exposed to direct sunlight. Avoid placing the cage close to a radiator or stove, too.
• A rabbit's life rhythm is influenced by light. Especially in the winter, when the days are shorter and darker, it is important

that the cage not be in some gloomy corner, or the animal may become lethargic.

• Like other rabbits, dwarfs can withstand quite severe cold if they have a chance to get acclimated. But drafts are harmful, often causing the snuffles and other respiratory problems. Be careful not to cause drafts when you air the room. There are cold air currents near the floor, so raise the cage somewhat off the floor, perhaps placing it on a low table.

• Put the cage somewhere where it is not easily knocked over, and lock it well, because if the rabbit gets a chance to escape it may hurt itself when jumping to the floor.

• Rabbits have extremely sensitive ears, and a TV or radio can be torture for them. Not only does the loud sound we hear bother them, but they also suffer from being exposed to ultrahigh frequencies which are inaudible to us.

Indoor Runs

If your dwarf rabbit has to spend the bulk of his time in a cage, it is specially important to his well-being that you allow him out regularly. Domestic rabbits have learned to make do with very little space, but this kind of existence runs counter to their natural disposition and their need for exercise. Just watch your pet rabbit when you let him out of the cage, and see him leap and jump with joy. You'll be amazed at how fast he can move and how varied his behavior is. It gives you a chance to observe him with your children and see him do things he never does inside his cage.

If you have a room with no fancy carpets and no electric wires near the floor, you can let him run free there. Otherwise you will need some kind of run for him. One cheap and very practical solution is to get a collapsible, wooden, child's playpen. Perhaps someone you know has one that is not in use. All you need do is stretch fine wire mesh around the sides.

Eating feces is normal behavior for a dwarf rabbit. In fact, it is healthy because the kidney-shaped excretions from the cecum contain important B vitamins.

If your rabbit is house trained, you can just put a box in one corner. If he is not too reliable in this department and you don't want the floor of the playpen to get dirty, let your rabbit have his exercise time in the morning and/or evening before he eats. If you are the type of person who gets upset by a mess, line the bottom of the playpen. Newspapers are not much good for this purpose because they are too easily kicked out of place. Old flooring is a possibility, but it is too slippery to be ideal. Don't put down plastic because the rabbit might nibble on it. Plastic contains softeners that dissolve in the stomach and can pose a serious health threat.

I have a good reason for going into such detail on how to protect the floor of the rabbit's run. Most dwarf rabbits are sold to city people who have no yard and often no balcony available to them. If these pet rabbits don't take to house training—which is not uncommon (see page 20)—they often pay for this shortcoming by spending the rest of their lives inside a cage. These animals tend to die young of heart disease, not to mention atrophy of the spirit.

For years I have used straw mats with a sheet of plastic underneath, a combination that works very well. The mats of natural fiber, which are readily available at most stores that sell flooring, are inexpensive and don't slide around. Try it, and you'll see how pleased your rabbit is. The chemically untreated mats are reminiscent of the grassy ground; they are wonderful for hopping on and scratching; and they have a pleasant straw smell. Nor do you have to worry about the rabbit nibbling on them. In fact, it seems better that the rabbit indulge his need to gnaw here rather than somewhere else. Some people claim that a rabbit given enough hay, twigs, and dry bread to chew on will not be tempted to exercise his teeth on other items, but I wouldn't want to be held to such a promise. Many of these winning creatures develop almost beaverlike habits and—curious as they are—want to test just about anything with their teeth.

Housing a Rabbit on the Balcony

If you have an apartment with a balcony, let your rabbit enjoy it, too. Let him have his daily run on the balcony, or set up house for him there from early spring to late fall. If you let the rabbit out just for his exercise period, make sure he's not likely to suffer a temperature shock. You can't put a coddled indoor rabbit out on a cold balcony from one day to the next. Get him used to outdoor temperatures gradually, and start when the days and nights are getting warmer.

Moving your rabbit to the balcony requires some forethought and preparation. If the balcony walls are not solid but have bars, you have to make sure the rabbit cannot slip through them. Use wire mesh that you attach solidly to the floor and that reaches up 32 inches (80 cm). If you don't like the looks of wire mesh, decorate or disguise it according to your tastes. If the floor is made of cold concrete, put down some of the straw mats I mentioned earlier or some leftover carpeting. In the height of summer it is important that the rabbit have a shady corner, because dwarf rabbits do not withstand the direct sun.

If your rabbit spends the night outdoors, too, he will need a small hutch for sleeping. One like the model shown in the drawing on page 18 is easy to construct. Set it up in such a way that the slope of the roof faces the predominant wind and rain direction. Build the hutch out of 3/4-inch, waterproof plywood, and make the floor area about 14 by 14 inches (35 x 35 cm). This way the rabbit will have enough room to move around, yet the space will stay warm enough in cooler weather. If the hutch is too large, the heat loss is too great.

The roof should be covered with a good grade of roofing felt or tar paper, and it should extend about 4 inches (10 cm) beyond the walls. Attach it with hinges so that you can flip it up. This is important because otherwise you cannot change the bedding. For the floor it is best to use something with a synthetic, waterproof surface that will not absorb urine and is easy to keep clean. An entry hole (about 6 inches [15 cm] in diameter; for larger crossbred animals, 7½ inches [18 cm]) is sawed into the front wall; locate it about 4 inches (10 cm) from the floor to prevent drafts. Of course, you can also buy ready-made rabbit hutches.

If you like to keep the door to the balcony open during the summer but want the rabbit to stay outside, construct a low gate to fit into the door opening. Simply build a wooden frame the width of the door opening and about 32 inches (80 cm) tall, then stretch wire netting over it.

A Home in the Garden

The ideal place for a dwarf rabbit is, of course, the garden or yard. Let your rabbit hop around there as much as possible, but stay close by because of dogs and cats. If you want to leave your dwarf rabbit outside without supervision, build a pen like the one shown on the right. But because rabbits like to dig, bury the wire mesh in the ground about 12 inches (30 cm) deep if you are setting up a permanent pen. For sleeping, build a hutch as described on page 17, but

A run and a sleeping box you can build yourself. This movable run is 32 inches tall, 40 inches wide, and about 5 feet long (80 x 100 x 150 cm). The weatherproof sleeping box has a roof that lifts up and a round entry hole.

cover not only the roof but also the walls with tar paper or roofing felt to keep out the rain. As protection against moisture from below, have a waterproof, insulating layer underneath the floor and raise the hutch off the ground on a couple of slats.

The Litter

An excellent litter for dwarf rabbits is the special small-animal litter that is available in pet stores and that consists of pressed sawdust or a mixture of peat and sawdust. You can use cat litter for your rabbit's litter box, but it is not suitable for the cage. It is too hard, and your rabbits can rub their paws raw on it. If the sides of the plastic pan are high enough, the litter will not be kicked out of the cage. If you keep a number of dwarf rabbits, you'll save a lot of money by periodically getting a load of straw from a farmer. For indoor cages, straw with a thick layer of newspapers underneath is the softest, cheapest, and most natural form of litter. In the fall you can also collect dry leaves (but not next to highways because of the poisonous exhaust fumes). Dwarf rabbits like to nibble on them, and the leaves, spread out on the cage floor, give off a pleasant, woodsy smell that permeates the entire room.

Food and Water Containers

The food dish should be made from heavy earthenware. The inside curve of these dishes (see drawing on page 30) is designed in such a way that the food is not kicked out easily, and they are so heavy that they are impossible to knock over. Almost all commercial cages come with a small hay rack that can be fitted to a wall inside the hutch. If yours doesn't have one, buy one (see Hay, the Basic Staple, page 25).

Make sure your rabbit *always* has water. Some dwarf rabbits get along with little water if they are given enough fruit, greens, and other vegetables, but others drink regularly, sometimes up to 1½ cups a day. Don't bother with a water bowl in an indoor cage. The water gets dirty, and the bowl—especially if it's made of plastic—will inevitably tip over. The best solution is an automatic water dispenser (the so-called gravity-fed bottle) that can be hung on the cage wall. When you buy one of these, ask for a model with a double-ball valve; the others usually drip constantly.

The Litter Box

If you attempt to house-train your dwarf rabbit (see page 20), you will need a box for him to use. Pet stores sell cat litter boxes that work very well for dwarf rabbits. But any plastic pan about 10 by 14 inches (25 x 35 cm) will do. I have turned the bottom tray of an old, discarded cage into a rabbit toilet. To make the cleaning easy, put a layer of newspaper underneath the kitty litter.

Transport and Nest Boxes

For occasions when you don't want to take the regular indoor cage on a trip or carry it on a visit to the veterinarian, you'll find special transport boxes useful. I always use them when I travel with my dwarf rabbits. You can order these boxes from a supply house for rabbit breeders or get one from a breeder you know.

Those who think they might want to let their female dwarf rabbit raise a family just once or twice should buy or build a nest box. When does have their first litter, they tend to be nervous and will feel safer in the dark inside such a box. In some ways it resembles the burrows of wild rabbits. A nest box—which you can easily build yourself—can also double as a rabbit house to be put in the indoor cage.

The Rabbit Leash

If you contemplate outings with your dwarf rabbit, you will need a leash (see page 22), especially at first. If the animal is not yet entirely used to you, or if it finds itself in a totally new environment, it might respond to a startling incident by running away. Once loose, the rabbit is not likely to come back in a hurry. And just try catching a nervous, excited rabbit! Pet stores sell cat leashes and collars (or harnesses) made of soft leather; these work fine for dwarf rabbits, too. Just punch a couple of extra holes to make the collar smaller and the fit will be perfect.

Keeping and Caring for a Dwarf Rabbit

Getting Settled

When you go to pick up your new dwarf rabbit, drive home with him directly, without stopping on the way. The cage at home should be ready—bottom covered with litter—and waiting in the spot designated for it. Place the newcomer in his cage gently, pet him, and talk to him reassuringly. Although the animal doesn't understand your words, your voice will have a soothing effect. Now withdraw a little, or sit quietly nearby, and let the rabbit sniff everything in peace. Always remember that an animal—no matter how young or old—needs some time to recover from the shock of being plucked from its familiar surroundings. It needs to get acquainted with its new home. That

Dwarf rabbits like to take a siesta now and then, and they should not be disturbed at these times.

is why you should not show off your new acquisition to all your relatives and friends right away, nor should the new member of the household be passed from one pair of small hands to the next. Children are usually much too excited at this point, so postpone the handling until later.

After a while you can put some food and water in the cage. Once the rabbit starts to eat and drink, and then perhaps to clean

itself, the initial shock is over. Give your dwarf rabbit a few days to get acquainted with his wider environment and sniff around (smelling is of primary importance to rabbits; see page 54). Pick him up now and then, put him on your lap, and pet him. This way he'll soon be at ease with everybody in the family. Dwarf rabbits need this kind of body contact. Each animal has its own special spot where it likes to be scratched, and you'll soon discover your pet's preference.

Don't plan an outing during the first few days. Too many new sights and experiences all at once would be overwhelming for the newcomer.

Can Dwarf Rabbits Be Housebroken?

You can tell by the heading that I don't subscribe to the theory that all rabbits can be housebroken if you only do it the right way. I think such claims are irresponsible and result in unhappiness for both animals and humans. Owners are vexed because their pets fail to live up to the claims made for them, and thousands of rabbits end up in animal shelters, or pay for their supposed shortcomings by spending the rest of their lives locked in cages, simply because their behavior does not conform to the promised standard.

My own dwarf rabbits are not all housebroken. At first I was disappointed, but now I simply vacuum up the few pellets that ''miss'' without worrying about it.

If you could look inside a wild rabbit burrow, you would see what orderly and neat creatures rabbits are. All the family members relieve themselves in the same spot. Domestic rabbits behave similarly; they don't leave droppings randomly all over the hutch. Make use of this inborn sense of cleanliness. Place a litter box in the rabbit's exercise pen from the very first day. Set the dwarf rabbit in it a few times; he may scratch in the litter, and if you're lucky he will get the idea. But many rabbits prefer to find their own spot—a corner of the room, under the sofa, behind a door, or next to a bureau—for "doing their business." There is not much you can do about it. But don't get upset, and especially don't scold or punish the little malefactor. Just pick up the dry, almost odorless, beanlike droppings; they can be removed without trace. Clean up a small puddle with warm water and mild soap. Now move the litter box to the spot the rabbit has selected. Cover well other places you want to protect. If you are lucky and have plenty of patience and persistance, your rabbit may get in the habit of using his box regularly.

How to Treat a Dwarf Rabbit Properly

The arrival of the new family member will mean some changes in your daily routine, and you will have to learn how to handle a dwarf rabbit properly.

Always remember that even a small creature like a dwarf rabbit needs not only food and basic care but also exercise, time out of the cage, and lots of affection. But there are also periods when the animal wants to be left alone. See if your rabbit is sleeping or wants to rest before you pet him or pick him up. And respect his rest by avoiding loud noises at those times. If you show no consideration you will provoke defense reactions (see page 52).

Dwarf rabbits don't always hold nice and still when you try to pick them up. Often they kick with all four feet and struggle to get free. If they fall or drop to the ground, they may hurt themselves. That is why it is important that you, as well as your children, get in the habit of grabbing and lifting the rabbit up properly. Never pull a rabbit up by its ears; that would be sheer cruelty. Reach with your right hand for the loose skin behind the neck and between the shoulder blades, and take a secure but not too tight hold. Don't be timid; get a good hold. If you don't grab enough skin, you'll only pull out the hair. Once you have a good hold, lift the rabbit up and support its behind with

This is how you should lift up a dwarf rabbit. Get a secure but not-too-tight hold of the loose skin between the shoulders, and support the rabbit's rear end with your other hand.

your left hand. This is very important, especially in the case of pregnant does. Now you're ready to carry the rabbit in your arms, but still keep one hand near the neck so that you could grab the animal again if it should attempt to jump down.

If you let your rabbit roam free in the apartment, open and close doors slowly.

Don't just burst into a room. And make sure there are no electric wires near the floor. Dwarf rabbits chew on these wires and can get electric shocks.

This is how you hold a dwarf rabbit properly. Place your free hand on the rabbit's back behind the head so that you can grip it if the animal should try to jump down.

The First Outing

A dwarf rabbit is not like a dog that you take out regularly or that accompanies you on longer walks. It will not hop along and keep up with you. Take your dwarf rabbit outdoors only if you have plenty of time. Sit down with him in a meadow, preferably in a spot that is far removed from traffic and not likely to be visited by dogs. If your rabbit doesn't race off but lies down flat on the grass with ears close to the head at the slightest unfamiliar sound, let him be. Everything is so new and overwhelming at first that it takes time for the realization of freedom to sink in and translate into joyful running and jumping. I get great pleasure out of simply sitting and watching my rabbits play outside. For me, observing the behavior and getting to know the different personalities of these quiet creatures is always a happy and refreshing break from the hectic pace of everyday life.

Leash or No Leash?

On your first few outings—and later if there is a chance that a dog might suddenly appear on the scene—it is advisable to take a leash along just in case. Otherwise it is better not to use one. A delicately built dwarf rabbit weighing two or three pounds requires a great deal of sensitivity on the part of the person holding the leash. Younger children, especially, tend to be impatient and pull or drag the animal in the direction it is supposed to go. But dwarf rabbits don't walk like people. They hop around, jump, and double back and forth; just try sometime to trace their course! They also like to dive under bushes, from whence they may be reluctant to reemerge and where you may not be able to follow them. But even here you shouldn't yank the animal back by the leash. It's best to prevent such situations. Pick up your dwarf rabbit at danger points and set him down again in a different part of the meadow.

A Play Corner for an Indoor Rabbit

Dwarf rabbits leading exclusive indoor lives—that is, if there is no balcony or yard available for them—need a chance to run free. But, unless there are "playmates," you will soon notice your rabbit getting bored even though he can move about at will. A smooth, flat floor where all he can do is hop back and forth does not offer much excitement. Rabbits love caves, hiding places in bushes and hedges, and grass or other low growth for cover. If you take your rabbit along to a spot in the country you can see that he never runs for a long time in the open. He keeps trying to hide behind you or under a bush. This behavior is instinctive, for if a rabbit moved much in the open it would be an easy target for raptors or martens.

It was my children who had the idea of making our rabbits' play corner more interesting. They got large and small cardboard boxes at the supermarket and set them up in the rabbit play area after having cut doors and windows in them. The dwarf rabbits were delighted with this innovation and immediately started hopping into and out of, on top of and over the boxes. Since then we have not seen our rabbits dozing out of sheer boredom anymore.

Grooming

Dwarf rabbits are among the cleanest pets. They wash themselves all over, including the ears, with great care. Their coat is always silky and smooth, unless an animal is sick. Only when a new coat is growing in do you have to use a slightly dampened chamois leather, a fine-toothed comb, or a soft brush on your rabbit. Brush both with the lie of the fur and occasionally against it. Many rabbits enjoy these brushings, which stimulate circulation, and they like to be brushed regularly any time of year.

Occasionally you'll find some dried discharge with a sweetish smell stuck in the fur around the genitals. Remove it gently with a cotton swab and some oil.

How to Clip the Toenails Properly

If your rabbit cannot wear down his toenails adequately in the yard or when running loose indoors, they will have to be trimmed

regularly. Overly long toenails seriously hamper the animal's movements. You can have the veterinarian or the pet dealer cut them, or you can try yourself. But it takes some expertise to cut them without touching nerve ends, especially if the animal has dark nails. And a good deal of skill is required in handling overly nervous animals.

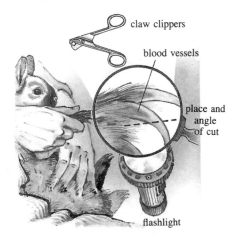

The proper way to clip the claws. Be careful not to cut into a blood vessel, and try not to splinter the nail (see enlarged inset). Hold the foot up against a strong light so that you can see the blood vessels better.

Have a helper. One of you can hold and pet the rabbit, while the other wields the nippers. (You can manage on your own, but it's that much harder.) Use special nippers (available at pet stores; see drawing page 23) or regular toenail clippers. It is a good idea to shine a bright light (flashlight) from below at the nails to be trimmed. This way you can see the central part of the nail better, where the nerves and blood vessels are. Be careful not to cut into the quick because this hurts and can cause bleeding. And don't try to cut the nails back too much. Probably you should let an expert (a breeder or pet dealer) demonstrate before you have your first go at it.

Checking the Teeth

It is important when you buy a rabbit to examine its teeth for proper bite. If there is a hereditary abnormality, you'll have to take the rabbit to the veterinarian every six to eight weeks to have the overly long teeth ground down. This is very unpleasant for everyone concerned. Unfortunately, overshot and undershot jaws and pincer bite have been getting more common in dwarf rabbits. Some possible reasons for this may be prolonged inbreeding, failure to cull animals with abnormal bite, and breeding for dwarf size.

Even if your rabbit has normal teeth, it is still a good idea to check the incisors occasionally to make sure they are getting enough wear. Rabbits need plenty of hay, branches, old bread, and other crunchy food (see page 26) because their teeth keep growing.

Cleaning of Cage and Accessories

Obviously, cleaning the cage and everything in it is part of taking care of your rabbit. Scrub the plastic tray at the bottom with hot water and a mildly scented household cleaner (remember the rabbit's sensitive nose), then wipe it dry. If you use newspaper underneath the litter, the cleanup will be easier. But check to see if your rabbit has a tendency to nibble on or eat the paper. If he does, you'll have to do without newspaper because printer's ink, which contains chemicals, is harmful to rabbits. Indoor cages should be cleaned twice a week, waterers and food dishes, daily. For hygienic reasons, the brushes used for the rabbit's dishes and water bottle should be reserved exclusively for this purpose.

If your dwarf rabbit should get sick, you have to clean the cage with a disinfectant to prevent reinfection through dirty litter. Disinfectant is also useful in preventive hygiene, but should not be used more often than every four to six months.

With a scent gland located under the chin, dwarf rabbits mark objects in their environment. The smell serves to define an animal's territory.

Diet

What Dwarf Rabbits Eat

Dwarf rabbits eat things that grow. Tidbits of meat or sausage, chocolate cake, and candy should therefore not be included in their diet; they are harmful to rabbits. In nature, rabbits find plenty of variety. The little gourmets have a choice of all kinds of plants, buds, leaves, and bark, and they eat berries and other fruit, mushrooms, and occasionally a small bug. Your pet dwarf rabbit needs a similarly varied and nutritious diet.

Wild rabbits don't suffer from deficiency diseases because they eat such a variety of things. And in nature the change from one kind of food to another, accompanying the gradual change of the seasons, is never sudden. Thus the sensitive digestive system of the animals is spared the jolt of an abrupt changeover. If you want your rabbit to stay in good health, keep these things in mind when deciding what to feed your pet (see Rules for Feeding, page 29).

Commercial Rabbit Food

Pet stores sell commercial food for dwarf rabbits that is of good quality and, if purchased in bigger packages, quite economical. These grain mixtures are usually composed of whole kernels and flakes of various grains (wheat, oats, rye, corn), buckwheat, oilseeds, various smaller seeds, and pellets. The modern pellet, which supplies all normal nutritional requirements, contains alfalfa meal, ground yellow corn, soybean meal, cottonseed meal, wheat middlings, ground peanut hulls, cane molasses, and sucrose, enriched with vitamins, minerals, some roughage, animal proteins, milk fat, and trace elements. These should always be present in a good grain mixture.

Give your dwarf rabbit some high-quality commercial food every morning (see Suggested Feeding Plan, page 30).

Hay, the Basic Staple

Your dwarf rabbit may and should have hay available year round, summer as well as winter. Put enough in the hay rack to last for the day and the night. Hay not only supplies roughage as an aid to digestion but, in addition to the bulk, also contains calcium and magnesium. Never feed damp or moldy hay. A sign of its freshness is if the hay is still fragrant and not too dusty. Don't use hay fresh from the field; it has to ripen for about six weeks.

The wrong kind of food and a lack of exercise lead to obesity. Dwarf rabbits that are too fat suffer from serious heart and circulatory problems which often lead to premature death.

Good hay consists of sweet grasses and clover; it is even better if other herbs are mixed in. You can buy high-quality hay at pet stores. If you need larger amounts, buy a bale of good hay from a first cutting directly from a farmer. Hay from a second cutting, being finer and thus easily digestible, is especially suitable for baby rabbits.

Greens and Succulent Foods

Greens and succulent foods (vegetables and fruit) are not only what a rabbit would naturally eat, but they are also the most healthful foods. However, there are a few things to remember: Never give too much at once; always also provide hay; and change over gradually from a diet of predominantly dry food.

Greens are highly nutritious and especially rich in protein and calcium. From spring to fall, you can collect greens on your walks; be careful, however, as many areas may have been treated with pesticides. When things cease growing outside, give your rabbit some of the fruit, greens, and other vegetables you eat. Here is a list of what your rabbit should eat and what should be avoided.

Wild plants you can gather

Desirable: Dandelion greens (in limited quantities), alfalfa, groundsel (has a slight laxative effect but stimulates molting), sainfoin, serradella, shepherd's purse, cow-parsnip, sow-thistle (excellent for pregnant does and litters), dock (particularly sorrel dock), borage, young nettles (also dried), common and English plaintain, bindweed, grasses, chickweed, pigweed, orache, watercress, and yarrow. (Only collect plants that you know and recognize.)

Less desirable (causes bloating): Red clover.

Poisonous (do not feed): Autumn crocus, all varieties of foxgloves, blue and trailing lobelia, privet, rhubarb, fool's parsley, poison hemlock, deadly nightshade, laburnum, and yew.

Greens and succulents from your garden or kitchen

Desirable: Carrots, carrot tops, endive, chicory, corn salad, raddish leaves, sweet corn, kale, kohlrabi, kohlrabi leaves, apples, pears, spinach, and herbs such as sage, parsley, peppermint, balm, and camomile.

Less desirable (give only in small amounts and check reaction; often cause bloating): Raw potatoes (without shoots), cauliflower, Brussels sprouts, all varieties of cabbage, lettuce, swedes (yellow turnips or rutabagas), and turnips.

Poisonous (do not feed): Raw beans, potato shoots.

Important reminder: Environmental poisons are a serious hazard for your dwarf rabbit. They harm your pet as much as they do you if not more so because of his smaller size. Never pick grasses or other plants along the roadside. Anything growing along highways is polluted by exhaust fumes (especially lead). If you collect plants in public parks, avoid locations where dogs urinate and defecate; plants from such places could carry disease agents.

If you cannot buy untreated fruit and vegetables, peel and wash everything well. If at all possible, collect plants from meadows away from cultivated fields and fruits and vegetables from gardens where no herbicides and insecticides are used. American fanciers must be very cautious when buying dried hay which is not wrapped commercially by a reputable company, as it may contain the highly toxic milkweed. This weed only grows in the United States. After eating it, the rabbit becomes paralyzed, drops its head between the forelimbs (the reason why this affliction is often called "head down disease"), and often arches its back. See your veterinarian immediately.

A six-week-old White-tipped Black dwarf rabbit. The white-tipped guard hairs are especially prominent in this youngster.

Diet

Foods for Nibbling

Just as a duck needs water for swimming, a dwarf rabbit has to have things to chew on. Its teeth never stop growing and have to be worn down continually. So supply your rabbit with hay and grain, and now and then give it some stale bread, hard crackers, or a special "nibbling mix" you can buy at pet stores (see page 30). The bread should be bone hard, free of mold, and without added salt or spices. Your little pet will be ecstatic if you bring him some beech, hazelnut, or maple twigs from a walk, or if you give him twigs of unsprayed fruit trees from your garden. If you bring in frozen twigs in the winter, let them thaw first. Your rabbit also appreciates certain twigs left over from pruning. Remember, however, that many garden trees and shrubs are poisonous (laburnum, privet, yew, thornapple, and so on).

Vitamins and Minerals

Rabbits are vegetarians; the food they eat—vegetable proteins, carbohydrates, and fats—is transformed through chemical processes in the body into animal proteins and fats. For this process to work properly, certain substances have to be present, namely vitamins and trace elements. Protein is crucial for the entire metabolism. But the need for protein is even greater for animals that are shedding (molting) and growing new coats, for young animals that are still growing, for pregnant and lactating females, and for bucks acting as studs.

Young purebred dwarf rabbits.
Above left: A Red female (5 weeks old). Above right: A Japanese male (1 year old). Below: Siamese dwarf rabbits (both 12 weeks old; buck on the left, doe on the right).

Your dwarf rabbit gets the necessary minerals and trace elements if he is given enough fresh foods along with his daily hay ration. Vitamins are absorbed by the body only in minute quantities, but if there is any deficiency, it may result in inhibited growth or other health problems. That is why a varied diet of a high-quality grain mixture and plenty of greens and succulent plants is so important.

Drinking Water

A dwarf rabbit should *always* have drinking water available. This is especially important on hot days and also in dry, heated rooms. If you fill an automatic water dispenser every day with fresh water (see drawing on page 30), the rabbit can drink whenever and how much it wants. (The bottle has to be cleaned regularly to prevent the growth of algae.) Many rabbits don't need any water at all if they eat enough juicy foods, but others on the same diet like to drink water. Healthy rabbits never drink more than what their system needs.

Rules for Feeding

• Keep the diet varied.
• When feeding greens and succulent foods, don't overdo it by giving too much all at once.
• Only give as much food as your dwarf rabbit can finish. Never leave fresh food lying around in the cage. It could wilt, ferment, rot, or grow mold. Spoiled vegetable matter can cause severe health problems (Diarrhea, see page 31).
• Never feed anything straight from the refrigerator, and avoid frozen vegetables (there are plenty of fresh vegetables and fruits available all year round, see page 26).

- After washing vegetables and fruits, shake the water off and let them drip well.
- Don't switch suddenly from one kind of food to another (for example, in the spring when you change over from dry to fresh foods). This is especially important in the case of young animals. They are often so eager for the fresh food that their eyes are indeed larger than their stomachs. If they overeat, particularly on things that bloat, death may be the consequence (see Tympanites, page 32). Rabbits, unlike humans, cannot vomit.
- Dwarf rabbits, like people, are subject to weight problems. Dwarf rabbits often get obese as a consequence of improper diet, lack of exercise, or genetic factors aggravated by breeding. These animals develop ugly rolls of fat. They get lazy; their bellies hang low; they puff and gasp for breath at the slightest exertion; and finally they succumb prematurely to degenerative heart disease. There is only one remedy: lots of exercise and a radical cutback on food. If this doesn't do the trick, introduce a weekly fast day of nothing but water and hay.

Feeding Times

Feed at regular intervals, preferably twice daily. Only does and baby rabbits need to eat three times a day. Train yourself to establish and stick to a routine so that the animal can develop a daily rhythm. Plan feeding times for the morning and late afternoon or early evening. If you pet and talk to your rabbit every time you feed him, he will jump with joy each time you approach with the food. This not only deepens your friendship, but also keeps feeding from becoming a mere mechanical chore.

Suggested Feeding Plan

Morning: A handful (3/4 to 1 ounce, or 20–25 g) of commercial rabbit food and perhaps a slice of apple or pear to add variety to your pet's diet.

Afternoon or evening: One handful of greens and succulent foods. In the summer, prefera- bly sow or milk thistle, dandelion greens, herbs, shepherd's purse, or clover (see Wild Plants You Can Gather, page 26), plus a piece of carrot or kohlrabi. In the winter sim- ply give one handful of whatever you have around for your own meals: lettuce, endive, chicory, etc. (see Greens and Succulents from Your Garden or Kitchen, page 26).

Daily: Hay or dry alfalfa—always put enough in the rack to last for 24 hours. Fill the water dispenser with fresh water.

Once or twice a week: Things to nibble on (the more variety, the better); for instance, twigs; in the fall, dry leaves (don't pick them up along roads with traffic), crunchy old bread crusts, and various products pet stores sell.

The drinking water stays nice and clean in an automatic water dispenser. Dwarf rabbits quickly learn how to use the device. In the foreground is a food dish that won't tip over.

Health Care and Diseases

Prevention is the Best Cure

Dwarf rabbits are naturally hardy, modest in their demands, and tough. With proper and conscientious care, a healthy rabbit without hereditary predisposition to disease will only rarely get sick. But there are periods of physical stress when special attention is needed. An animal's resistance is lowered when its body is subject to more than the normal demands. This is the case when the animal is young, when a doe is pregnant or lactates, when the new coat grows in, as well as when there is a sudden change in climate or temperature.

The best prevention—which is the crucial factor in keeping rabbits healthy—is to set up living conditions that take the animal's natural needs into account and to follow the advice on keeping and care outlined in the previous chapters.

First Symptoms of Illness

If you spend time regularly with your dwarf rabbit, you'll quickly notice any change in behavior or appearance (see Signs of Health and of Disease, page 35). Does your rabbit come hopping to the gate happily as soon as he sees you bringing food? Is his appetite good, and is he active and lively? Is his digestion normal, and is there no sign of diarrhea? Does his fur lie flat to the body, and is it smooth and glossy? Are his eyes alert, and do the ears respond to sounds? Or does he sit listlessly and hunched up in a corner, perhaps with flattened ears, a dull, staring look in his eyes, the sides of the body caved in or visibly distended, and the coat rough? Does he keep scratching himself, is his breathing irregular, or is he behaving abnormally in some other way? If you keep a careful eye on your rabbit, you'll spot any potential problem in good time—the earlier, the better.

Diseases That Can Occur in Dwarf Rabbits

Diarrhea

Causes: Sudden change in diet from dry to fresh food; food that is spoiled or too cold; greens contaminated with chemicals. Also, disorders of the stomach and intestines caused by drafts or damp bedding (especially serious for young animals). Diarrhea can also be a symptom of a cold. Remember, however, that diarrhea is not a disease, but rather, a sign of some other disease process in the body.

Symptoms: The droppings are soft to runny and smell foul or sour. The animal eats little or nothing, and soon loses strength. Blood in the feces is a serious sign.

Treatment: Disinfect the cage; wash food dishes and water container with hot water. Change the litter once or twice daily. Stop giving any greens or succulent foods, and feed only hay (second cutting is best) and some dry bread. Offer lukewarm camomile tea and some boiled, unsalted rice. If the diarrhea persists more than two days, consult the veterinarian immediately because prolonged diarrhea is life-threatening.

Constipation

Causes: Sudden changeover from fresh to dry food; too little or no water (lactating does always have to have plenty of water); insufficient exercise.

Symptoms: The rabbit stops eating and sits in the cage with its back hunched up high; sometimes the body is bloated and sensitive to the touch. Not enough stool is passed or, in severe cases, none at all.

Treatment: In a mild case of constipation, offer fresh water at room temperature (should be available to the rabbit at all times). When the animal shows some interest in food, offer endive or corn salad, as well as crunchy carrots. In more severe cases, give one teaspoon of olive oil or paraffin oil twice a day. If no feces are passed for two days, take the animal to the veterinarian. Replace the bedding with white paper towels, so that you can tell if and how much stool was produced. Rabbits that are fed conscientiously and have access to fresh water do not suffer from constipation.

Tympanites, Bloat, Scour, or Mucoid Enteritis

Causes: Wrong foods, such as red clover, or too much cabbage. This condition often affects young rabbits because their intestinal flora is not yet geared to adult food. (Young rabbits that were separated too early from their mother are at greatest risk; see page 14.) Another cause is poisoning from moldy hay or spoiled food. Sometimes tympanites accompanies infectious diseases.

Symptoms: Severe bloating of the body, caused by fermentation in the gastrointestinal tract; restlessness and grinding of the teeth, which are signs of severe pain; swollen and dull eyes; fur becomes tangled and rough. Sometimes there is persistent, violent drumming of the hind feet, shortness of breath (the stomach is pressing on the lungs), weak circulation, and a failing condition within a few hours. In the worst cases, the stomach or intestinal wall bursts, or the animal suffocates. Sudden and virulent cases of tympanites are fatal.

Treatment: Remove food and bedding at the first sign. Impose a day of fasting (no food of any kind, including hay), but be sure that there is plenty of fresh drinking water. Force-feed one or two teaspoons of caraway tea three or four times a day. Gently massage the lower body to help get rid of the gas-producing intestinal contents faster. A teaspoon of black coffee revives weak circulation (for full-grown animals; young

It is important to know what the different parts of a dwarf rabbit are called.

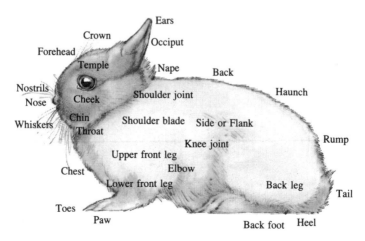

Ears
Crown
Occiput
Forehead
Temple
Nape
Back
Nostrils
Haunch
Nose
Cheek
Shoulder joint
Whiskers
Chin
Shoulder blade
Side or Flank
Throat
Knee joint
Rump
Upper front leg
Chest
Elbow
Lower front leg
Back leg
Toes
Tail
Paw
Back foot
Heel

rabbits should get no more than half a teaspoonful). Give a little bit of hay on the second day, and lots of water.

Important: If there is no relief on the second day, *consult a veterinarian.* If the symptoms are severe the first day, visit the veterinarian immediately!

When the symptoms have subsided, start feeding fine hay (from a second cutting), and *very gradually* shift back to the normal diet. Refrain for some time from giving foods that are hard to digest (this includes all brassica, as well as lettuce and raw potatoes). Proceed similarly whenever there is impaired stomach or intestinal functioning.

Snuffles

Causes: There are two kinds of snuffles: One is contagious and caused by virus or bacteria; the other is not contagious and may stem from irritation to the mucous membranes by dust—from hay or just dust in the air—or caustic cleaning agents. Contributing factors are a diet low in vitamins and improper conditions and housing.

Symptoms: Runny nose in both kinds of snuffles; also frequent sneezing. Infectious snuffles affect the general state of health (listlessness, lack of appetite, and "snorting"). The animal is unable to keep its nostrils clean of the sticky, yellowish nasal discharge, and the chest and front paws are often caked with mucus from unsuccessful attempts to wipe the nose.

Treatment: First move the animal to a dry but not too warm spot. Give multivitamin drops (available at pet stores) to improve general health, and administer a camomile steam bath. For this, place the rabbit in his (locked) cage, put a bowl of hot (but not boiling) water with some camomile flowers in front of it, and drape a cloth over both the cage and the bowl. Make sure the rabbit cannot get in contact with the hot tea. If the nasal discharge persists (whether watery or pussy), or if you notice changes in behavior, consult the veterinarian. Only a veterinarian can tell you how serious the problem is and what measures are appropriate for the case.

Heat Stroke

Causes: Build-up of heat in the body, caused by direct sun (during travel or if there is no shady corner in the cage or run); excessive heat (especially dangerous in the absence of drinking water).

Symptoms: Fast, shallow breathing, with the nostrils wide open and the entire body trembling. If relief is not provided quickly, the rabbit will die.

Treatment: Move the animal to the shade immediately. Offer water at room temperature, allow the rabbit to move freely, and cool first the head and then the legs with damp cloths. The cloths should be cool but never ice cold. To stimulate circulation, force-feed one teaspoonful of black coffee (only half a teaspoonful for young animals).

Eye Inflammations

Causes: Not every eye inflammation signals myxomatosis (see page 34). Inflammation of the conjunctiva, or mucous membrane lining the eyelids, inflammation of the tear duct, or inflammation of the cornea can have such common causes as dusty hay, dirt, drafts, colds, and injuries from fights. Usually only one eye is affected, although both eyes may become infected.

Symptoms: The rabbit keeps shutting the inflamed, tearing eye. The conjunctiva or the white part of the eye is reddened and sometimes swollen. The hairs around the eyes are sticky and caked together, because the eye pocket fills up with water that runs down the animal's cheek.

Treatment: Get a prescription for an eye ointment from your veterinarian. He can also determine the cause of the problem, which you should then eliminate.

Fractures

Causes: Broken bones can result if a dwarf rabbit is dropped, jumps out of someone's arms or out of the cage and lands badly, gets a foot caught (a frequent occurrence with young rabbits that get a foot stuck in the hay rack), is squashed by a closing door, or is accidentally stepped on.

Symptoms: The animal attempts to favor the injured limb, or it may sit in a corner, immobile and apathetic. Fractures are not always easy to detect.

Treatment: Only a veterinarian can determine whether and what kind of treatment is necessary.

Coccidiosis

Causes: This disease is caused by Coccidia, microscopic protozoa that live in the epithelium of the intestines and destroy it. Dirty bedding is a prime factor in spreading this rabbit disease.

Symptoms: A bloated body, as in the case of tympanites (see page 32), but accompanied by diarrhea. If the infestation is heavy, the rabbit's strength declines rapidly.

Treatment: Isolate the affected animal immediately so that other rabbits will not get contaminated through contact with the droppings of the sick animal. Disinfect the cage thoroughly (Lysol™). (Never use the contaminated bedding as manure in the garden.) The parasites remain viable for up to eighteen months and survive extremely

cold temperatures down to $-60°$ F ($-50°$ C). Immediate treatment by a veterinarian is necessary. Take along a stool sample.

Mange

Cause: Mange can occur on the body, the head, or the ears. It is caused by different kinds of mites that penetrate the inner layers of the skin.

Symptoms: The affected areas show loss of fur and reddening of the skin; later, scales and smeary, crusty scabs form. The rabbit keeps scratching and thus spreads the mange. Tilting and violent shaking of the head signal the presence of ear mites.

Treatment: Start treatment as soon as you notice the problem. Mange is highly contagious. Isolate the affected animal and keep cage and equipment meticulously clean. Caution: Scabs will fall off into the bedding. Remove both scabs and bedding from the cage and burn them.

Myxomatosis

Cause: This disease was first noted in Germany in 1953, and since then has wiped out entire populations of wild rabbits. Myxomatosis is caused by a virus that is transmitted by bloodsucking insects (for example, mosquitoes). If you keep your dwarf rabbit indoors and only occasionally on the balcony, you don't need to worry about this disease. The danger of infection is greatest for rabbits that are kept in hutches near wild rabbit populations (especially in wet areas and river valleys).

Symptoms: Two to five days after contracting the virus the animal develops teary eyes and boils on the head and genitals. Shortly thereafter the boils break open, and the

Health Care and Diseases

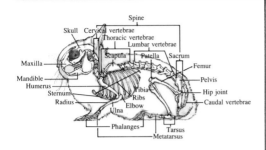

The skeleton of a dwarf rabbit. Knowing the names of the various bones can be useful in conversations with your veterinarian.

discharge of pus, which sticks to food and bedding, causes further infection. In the later stages, boils occur all over the body;

the animal loses weight, has difficulty breathing, and dies within a few days. Treatment: There is no remedy for this disease. Preventive measures include vaccination in areas where the disease is widespread (effective for six months) and keeping out mosquitoes (replace wire mesh in hutches with fine screening and use the old-fashioned fly strip, which is coated with a sticky substance). Some rabbits do survive the disease and are then immune to it for the rest of their lives, though scars and perforated ears remain as an ugly memento. Attending to the sick rabbit with conscientious care, keeping cage and other items immaculately clean, and eliminating mosquitoes all improve the chance of recovery.

Signs of Health and of Sickness

	Healthy Rabbits	Sick Rabbits
Coat	Smooth and glossy; fur lies flat. There are no bare spots or signs of parasites.	Dull and rough; fur is ragged and sticks out; bald spots, scales, and scabs.
Skin	Very elastic; is easy to get hold of when one picks up the rabbit.	The usually loose skin is stretched tightly across the back.
Ears	React instantly to noises; are very clean and free of wounds; active movement.	Little movement; folded back; gritty surface inside; swellings, formation of nodes.
Eyes	Clear, warm, shiny, expressive; react clearly to changes in light.	Rigid, fixed stare, dull, glassy look; teariness.
Nose	Dry, sometimes slightly moist (as in very dusty air); mucous membrane: pale pink, well supplied with blood; even rising and falling of nostrils (faster in heat).	Watery or slimy to pussy discharge; sneezing and snorting, bluish discoloration, accelerated breathing; nostrils wide open.
Teeth	Normal length, correct bite (see drawing on page 32).	Overgrown, bent into hornlike or ringlike shapes; faulty bite (see page 24).
Belly	Completely clean; belly is roundish but not bloated, nor are the sides caved in.	Fur sticky or encrusted with excreta; belly is hard and bloated (pregnant does, of course, have an enlarged abdomen); diarrhea; droppings not pelletlike but a shapeless mush.

Dwarf Rabbits as Patients

There is hardly a quieter and more long-suffering patient than a dwarf rabbit. It does not whimper, whine, or complain even when in extreme pain. Only the look in the eyes betrays suffering, and changes in behavior and appearance indicate illness.

Please remember always that it is your responsibility to provide proper care for a pet that is sick. Don't try to play doctor. You should initiate treatment without the advice of a veterinarian only in a case of acute emergency or if the ailment is not serious and has a simple cure. But often the symptoms are practically interchangeable, so that it is hard for the layperson to diagnose a specific condition. Frequently a laboratory analysis (of a stool sample) is necessary. Generally you can be of greatest service to your sick rabbit—as well as to the veterinarian—if you observe your pet closely so that you can answer the following questions:

- What signs of illness did you notice?
- When did you first observe a change in behavior?
- Has the rabbit been eating? If yes, when, how much, and what?
- What are the droppings like? Does the animal have diarrhea or is it constipated?

Tell the veterinarian in as much detail as you can everything you have noticed. This will help him arrive at a diagnosis.

When looking after your little patient at home, follow the directions of the veterinarian and observe these few general rules:

- In case of all infectious diseases, change the bedding very frequently (sometimes it is best not to use bedding or litter at all), disinfect the cage (with Lysol™ in a dilution of ½ cup [4 oz] per gallon [3¾ liters] water), and wash food dishes and waterers with hot water.

- At any sign of illness, shift to easily digestible food, giving your rabbit fine hay, perhaps a piece of carrot, and a few greens (nothing that bloats). Make sure the surroundings are quiet, and protect the animal from all kinds of strains (for example, drafts and changes in temperature).

- Be patient if the animal appears distracted and perhaps even bites out of fear or pain. Understanding and sympathy are essential now.

- Patience is required if you have to give your dwarf rabbit tea or liquid medications. Use a teaspoon (a pipette or plastic syringe may be bitten in half). Get someone to hold the animal while you carefully pull down the lip on one side, put the teaspoon in the corner of the mouth, and let the liquid run in. (Don't let go of the animal until it has swallowed.)

Behavior patterns you will often observe. Above right: A Siamese dwarf rabbit rising up on its hind legs to get a better look. Above left: A Siamese dwarf rabbit grooming itself. Below: Dwarf rabbits getting acquainted through sniffing (Siamese buck on the left and Red doe on the right).

Breeding and Propagation

Controlled Breeding or Mere Propagation

A good breeder aims to produce not only healthy but also beautiful animals. Beautiful, when applied to dwarf rabbits, means that the animal conforms as closely as possible to the ideal as defined in the breed's standard of perfection. The commercial value of coat and meat is of little practical consideration in the case of dwarf rabbits. The breeder's main ambition is to exhibit his animals at shows and have them judged. Breeding rabbits this way involves keeping breeding records, tattooing the rabbits, breeding very selectively, and, inevitably, specializing in one color or kind of marking, for it often happens that only one out of thirty or forty baby rabbits is of show quality. Most breeders belong to a rabbit club, where members have a chance to share their experience and expand their knowledge.

There are also people who raise rabbits but are not interested in breed standards or in exhibiting their animals in shows. They are either hobby breeders who raise a litter for the pleasure of watching the baby bunnies grow up (many pet owners), or they raise rabbits for commercial reasons.

Some Terms You Should Be Familiar with

In exhibition catalogs and specialized publications you may come across terms and abbreviations that are not familiar to you.

Dwarf rabbits and Guinea pigs get along fine. The picture shows a Red dwarf rabbit and a bicolored Guinea pig.

Breeders' Lingo

Breeder	An adult rabbit used for propagation; also a person who keeps breeding rabbits
Buck	A male rabbit
Dewlap	Fold of loose skin under the chin of does
Doe	A female rabbit
Gestation	Period of 28 to 34 days from mating to kindling
Grade Rabbits	Rabbits that can be identified as to breed but do not have purebred parents
Heat	Period of time when the female is ready to mate
Hock	First joint of hind leg, thickly padded with fur
Junior	Rabbit under six months of age
Kindle	When a doe gives birth to a litter, she is said to kindle
Molting	Shedding fur in preparation for a new coat
Pair	Male and female to be mated to each other
Purebred Rabbits	Rabbits that can be traced back along their pedigrees for at least three generations
Registered Rabbits	Rabbits that can be traced back for more than three generations
Scrub Rabbits	Rabbits that cannot be identified as to their breed
Senior	Rabbit over six months of age
Variety	A group within a breed; identified by color or markings
Weaning	Separating the young from the doe, usually at six to eight weeks of age

In exhibition catalogs and in magazine advertisements some abbreviations are commonly used, as for instance 1,0, which means one buck; 0,1, which means one doe; 1,2, which means one buck and two does. The figure before the comma indicates the number of bucks, and the figure after the comma, the number of does.

All pedigreed rabbits have tattooed ears for identification. In the United States (where the regulations of the American Rabbit Breeders Association apply), the private identification number or mark goes in the left ear and the registration number, in the right. The British Rabbit Council uses a registration ring on a rabbit's hindleg for identification at shows. Such a ring is made of hard, light metal and is slipped over the rabbit's leg soon after it leaves the nest and is weaned. Each ring is embossed with the initials BRC, as well as the year that the ring is issued, and a letter to signify the group of breeds for which the ring should be used. For example, the Netherland dwarf rabbit wears a ring with the letter *X*, and a Polish, the letter *A*. It is understandable that these rings come in various sizes depending on the breed in question.

If you contemplate buying a dwarf rabbit at an exhibition, check how the animal was rated. Judges evaluate the entrants on a point system with 100 points as the maximum. A rabbit scoring 96 or 94 points would therefore be of excellent quality. In addition, prizes are awarded, such as Best of Breed, Best of Show, etc. (Any such distinctions earned are noted on a card that is attached to the rabbit's cage, and the breeder will give you written confirmation when you purchase the rabbit.)

Some Things to Consider before You Breed Your Dwarfs

It is a most natural occurrence for animals to mate and produce young. But keep in mind that you and your pets are not living in the wild but in the manmade environment of your home and garden. Here the size of populations is not naturally regulated by limited food supplies, size of territory, and predators. It is the owner who bears full responsibility for any animal living under human care.

The decision to raise a litter of baby bunnies often arises from a desire to incorporate a bit of nature into our lives. What is involved here is the pleasure of watching close up the biological processes of gestation and birth and, of course, the delight of having these cute, helpless, soft, and furry little creatures around to touch and see. But consider seriously whether you are set up to deal properly with your dwarf rabbit's offspring. Ask yourself the following questions ahead of time, so that your enjoyment will not later be spoiled by worrying about how you will dispose of the animals when they get bigger.

• Do you and your family really have enough time to look after the pregnant doe and later her offspring? Make sure there are no vacations or moves planned.

• Do you realize that the young animals will need space and cost money? You'll have to buy new cages or hutches for them because they cannot be kept with their mother indefinitely.

• Are you planning to give away the young rabbits? To whom? Find takers in good time who will treat dwarf rabbits properly and lovingly.

• How do your children feel about the idea? I notice again and again that children are not consulted in the decision to raise a rabbit family and that they are not prepared for the event. Later on there may be tears, and the parents may be confronted with feelings of their children that they, as adults, never gave any thought to.

Consider also the potential trauma of separation later on. We once had three baby dwarf rabbits named Susi, Mohrle, and Little Spot—names my children had selected before the bunnies were born—that we could not keep for lack of space. It was a great consolation to my children that we found good homes for these pets and that we were allowed to visit them occasionally in their new homes to check on their progress.

Choosing the Breeders

Nature occasionally takes us by surprise. What we thought were two female siblings may turn out to be something else, and offspring may be on the way before we quite realize our mistake. All you can do at that point is to make the best of it, enjoy the babies, and take good care of the family. But as a general rule we ''plan'' parenthood, and in this normal situation we should only mate animals that meet the following standards.

• Both parent animals must be completely healthy (that is, no hereditary diseases and no acute illnesses).
• The animals should not be molting when they are mated; this would place too great a strain on their physical system.
• The age of the breeders is important. Dwarf rabbits reach sexual maturity early— at twelve weeks (does and bucks should be housed separately from this point on)— but they are much too young for breeding then. Does that are mated too early may sustain permanent physical damage. The doe should be at least seven months old and the buck, eight months for a first mating.
• A conscientious breeder always makes sure that the buck is the same size or— better yet—slightly smaller than the doe, never the other way around. Otherwise the babies are too large and complications are likely at birth.

These basic rules apply equally to the fancier who is producing purebred animals and to the pet owner who only wants to raise one litter. If it is your ambition to breed a certain type of dwarf rabbit, then you should join a local rabbit breeders' club (see Useful Addresses, page 55). You will have to learn about genetics, pedigree records, how to buy purebred dwarf rabbits that serve your goals, and many other things, all of which require a lot of time and commitment.

The Mating

In dwarf rabbits, the ability to conceive is not tied to a season or cycle. The release of the egg is triggered by the act of mating. Ten hours after copulation, the doe's mature eggs descend from the ovary and are fertilized by the buck's sperm, which remains viable for twenty-five to thirty hours. Interest in mating can be stimulated by adding certain foods to the diet (for example, oats), changes in environment (room temperature), or by placing the doe in an empty hutch previously inhabited by a buck. According to recent research, the readiness to mate is also affected by light.

The mating should always take place in the buck's hutch—never in the doe's. She would defend her territory and might bite him badly. Also, the buck would want to mark his new surroundings profusely, and thus be distracted from his real business. On his own turf he feels secure and is not disconcerted by the doe's attacks. Occasionally, a doe refuses to have anything to do with a buck. (Respect her feelings and try with a different animal.) Usually, however, the buck's smell and his affectionate licking of her head and neck put her in the right mood. When copulating, the buck mounts the doe's back while she raises her rear end into a receptive position. After ejaculating, he slides down her side, often with a short growling sound, and lies there for a few seconds, exhausted. I have quite often seen a buck circle a reclining doe a few times and finally settle next to her and lick her lovingly.

In most cases one mating suffices, although in nature repeated matings are common.

Gestation and Birth

During the four weeks following the mating you may notice some real changes in your doe. Animals that were peaceful and friendly become nervous and may occasionally scratch and bite, something they had not done before. Others that were nervous and fidgety before tend to calm down and seem almost phlegmatic. All pregnant does display an instinct peculiar to their species from the sixth day on: They start scratching their bedding, trying to burrow into whatever is available and build a nest. Give your doe lots of hay or straw even if you don't do so ordinarily. A small kindling or nest box also

enhances your rabbit's sense of well-being, because she will feel safer in a cavelike space.

Above all, make sure she has peace and quiet and is spared all discomfort. Lift her up only if absolutely necessary, and when you do, support her body immediately with your other hand (see page 21). Don't grab her by the skin and leave her dangling in the air. During the period of gestation, be especially conscientious to feed her a nutritious and well-balanced diet and to keep her supplied with fresh drinking water. At this time it is also appropriate to give her calcium supplements and vitamins (available at pet stores).

The gestation period of dwarf rabbits is from twenty-eight to thirty-one days. In the case of babies bred for very small size, gestation can extend to thirty-three days. This has something to do with a birth hormone that requires a longer period for the development of the fetuses. False pregnancies are also not unknown in dwarf rabbits. Does with this condition display all the behavior patterns typical of a pregnant animal, digging restlessly in the bedding, running around with straw in their mouths, building nests, and pulling out their wool. But they usually start all this very soon after the mating, whereas does that have conceived wait until the last quarter of their pregnancy to build their nests and pull their wool. I had one dwarf doe that didn't start pulling wool until the very last day. One sure sign of pregnancy is the visible swelling in the fourth week of the mammary glands and the abdomen. Observe your doe carefully (especially if she lives in an outdoor hutch), so you will be ready to assist right after the birth if there is any need for it. Sometimes a doe neglects to tuck her babies into the warm wool nest, leaving them strewn all over the hutch. This may happen if the doe has suffered great pain during kindling, if there was some interference, or after an exceptionally long gestation. In such a case move the little ones into the nest immediately, or they will die of the cold.

Does assume a squatting position to give birth. Everything happens very quickly, and usually there are no problems. If a baby gets stuck in the birth canal, the doe tries to pull it out and sometimes injures it in the process. It's not that the animal intends to hurt her young but simply that the pain makes her bite harder than necessary to get a hold of the baby that is stuck. As soon as the babies are born, the mother licks the naked, blind creatures dry, bites through the umbilical cord, and eats the afterbirth, so that the nest stays clean. Occasionally it happens that a baby rabbit gets partially or entirely eaten in the process. Opinions about what causes this behavior vary. Some experts cite vitamin deficiency, while others suspect that the mother gets carried away licking, noticing too late or not at all that she has already removed the amniotic sac.

Purebred dwarf rabbits usually have litters of only two to four babies, but a conscious effort is being made to select breeding stock that will produce litters of five or six.

Shortly after the kindling, carefully perform a nest check. Lure the mother out of the hutch with a special food treat, so that you can examine the nest in peace. Carefully push the hay and wool aside a little, and make sure all the young are alive and uninjured. If there are remains of afterbirth or stillborn animals, these have to be removed. Wash your hands thoroughly before reaching into the nest, but don't use a strongly scented soap. Dwarf rabbits have

A doe nursing her young. A rabbit mother does not lie down to nurse; instead she sits in a squatting position and the young lie on their backs under her belly.

extremely sensitive noses (see page 54), and strange smells might upset the new mother.

The Development of the Young

Just two days after giving birth to two little bunnies, our Thuringian dwarf Mümmi was her old self again. The irritability that had characterized her pregnancy disappeared. She let us pet her again and clearly enjoyed it, and she spent most of her time, except for her daily run, lying peacefully in front of the nest box. I fed her two to three times a day while she nursed her babies, and I made sure that her water dispenser was always filled with fresh water.

Dwarf does that are nursing perform an amazing job keeping up with the appetite of the baby rabbits, for within a week after birth these little creatures double their weight. After all, it takes a human baby about half a year to accomplish a comparable weight gain. This makes you realize how important it is that the doe be given a well-balanced and nutritious diet with plenty of water. Nature is always primarily concerned with the survival of new life. The doe needs more nutrients and vitamins than she ordinarily gets to satisfy the needs of her young. If she doesn't get enough, she starts using up her own reserves and becomes emaciated.

Dwarf rabbits, like their relatives living in the wild, come into this world naked, deaf, and completely helpless. They are slow to develop. Their eyes don't open until the seventh to ninth day, and the covering of little down grows into a thick coat very slowly. As truly nidiculous creatures (that is, spending the first part of life in a nest), they stay hidden in the warm wool nest for eighteen to twenty-one days, and for four to five weeks they live almost exclusively on mother's milk, which is high in both fat and protein. Don't take the little bunnies out of their nest prematurely because you are curious or impatient. The mother rabbit herself will determine when the time is ripe. The doe's lactating pattern allows the sensitive intestines of the young to have a chance to adjust to solid food. She produces the greatest quantity of milk between the twelfth and fifteenth day of nursing, and after the sixth week, she dries up rapidly. You will be amazed at how quickly and eagerly the young bunnies start eating alongside their mother. Between the sixth and the seventh week they will be independent enough to be given away.

Stillbirths and Death of the Doe

Unfortunately it is not uncommon for dwarf rabbits to be stillborn. Premature rabbits with a gestation period of less than twenty-eight days are generally not viable, and delayed births thirty-three days or more after the mating often produce stillbirths, too.

A hormone that inhibits growth and thus produces dwarf size is responsible for these dead litters. The more marked the dwarf features are—as in the case of show animals—the more likely this hormone will lead to stillborn litters. This is the reason why a prize-winning exhibition doe is not necessarily a good breeder. It often turns out that mating a less spectacular doe with a prize, top-ranking buck produces the best litters, and the doe also raises them more conscientiously.

If a mother rabbit dies during the first twelve days after giving birth, the prognosis for the young is bleak. If the doe dies later, chances of survival are better. If you don't know of another lactating doe that might nurse the orphaned bunnies, try to raise them on cat milk, which most closely resembles rabbit milk in composition, or on baby formula. Gradually you can add strained oat gruel, carrot juice, and vitamins. But don't underestimate the commitment involved in being a foster mother. It takes a great deal of patience to teach a baby bunny to drink from a bottle. The babies have to have three to five feedings a day, which have to be followed by gentle massaging of the abdomen to stimulate digestion (the doe licks her young after every meal). Then, of course, the nursery needs to be kept clean. And the baby rabbits like to be warm; they are comfortable at about 86° F (30° C). This means that the room has to be well heated, or you can put a thickly wrapped hot-water bottle under the nest. If you do succeed in bringing up the little ones, your efforts will be well rewarded. Often dwarf rabbits that have been hand raised are exceptionally affectionate.

Dwarf Breeds and Color Varieties

Show animals are judged according to guidelines established by the Standard Commission, (see What a Purebred Dwarf Rabbit Should Look Like, page 13). The ideal picture we have of dwarf rabbits—their weight, body shape, build, and ears—are the same for all breeds except lop-eared dwarf rabbits. The main contents of the descriptions that follow indicate the color and markings of the fur and the color of the eyes and claws of some of the more popular dwarf rabbit varieties.

White Dwarf Rabbit or Polish Rabbit

Blue-eyed White (BEW) and Red- or Ruby-eyed White (REW): The Red-eyed White dwarf rabbit is the oldest dwarf breed (the first seventeen "Poles" were shown at Hull, England, in 1884) and is consequently the "purest" strain. Among REWs we find the top-ranking animals with the shortest well-rounded ears (not longer than 2½ inches [6 cm]) and the most "cobby" build. Red-eyed Whites can be traced back to pure white Polish rabbits that had been bred to create an imitation of or substitute for the expensive white ermine fur. This is reflected in the German name for white rabbits, *Hermelin-Kaninchen,* which means literally "ermine rabbits." After the turn of the century, the precursors of our dwarf rabbits as we know them today were imported from England to Germany (1903). In Germany, various dwarf strains were developed such as sables and smokes, self colors of black and blue, Himalayans, and silvers. They became increasingly popular after the First World War. Breeders did not succeed in breeding Blue-eyed White rabbits until 1918, although it took a long time before these animals resembled the breed standard as closely as

their red-eyed counterparts. The first Blue-eyed "Hermelins" were seen at the famous World Exhibition in Leipzig, Germany, in 1919.

Contact sniffing. Dwarf rabbits engage in an intensive, mutual investigation to determine whether they like each other.

Coat color: Pure white with a definite sheen. There may be no yellow cast to the coat or gray tinge or stains. Whiskers (or vibrissae) white.
Claws: Translucent.
Eyes: REW—without pigment, that is, albino eyes, which are a bright red, not pale or sullen; BEW—light blue.

Colored Rabbits

The coat color of dwarfs is the same in all respects as that of larger breeds or races of that color. In addition to the following varieties a number of new ones have recently been developed. More are to be expected! For more information, contact the American Netherland Dwarf Rabbit Club (see page 55).

Color Varieties
Black: See color photo on page 48.
Coat color: Coal black on all parts of the body. No rusty tinge or light spots permitted

Dwarf Breeds and Color Varieties

(The under color is a pure dark slate blue as in the Alaska rabbit). Whiskers black.
Claws: Dark (blackish brown).
Eyes: Dark brown.

Red: See color photos on front cover and on pages 28, 37, 38, and 48.
Coat color: A rich fox red on all parts of the body with a lighter shade (yellowish; not white, which is considered a flaw) on the rim around the eyes, on the jowls, the chin, the inside of the legs, the belly, and the underside of the tail. Whiskers dark yellowish brown.
Claws: A dark horn color.
Eyes: Brown.

Havanna: See color photos on back cover and on page 10.
Coat color: A rich dark brown (chestnut) on all parts of the body, without gray or rusty tinge. The under color is blue. In this color variety the luster of the coat is especially important because it helps bring out the color. Whiskers brown.
Claws: A dark horn color.
Eyes: Dark brown (with a reddish glow).

Chinchilla
Coat color: Laypeople often call this rabbit gray, but the color is an interplay of many different shades. If you look at a single hair you will see an under color, an intermediate band, and a cover color, each of which has to be clearly distinct. The under color is blue, the intermediate band whitish with a black little ring, and the cover color a light ash gray. The back also has pure black and black-and-white hairs mixed in. The rims of the ears are black, and the underside of the tail is white, as is the cover color of the belly. Whiskers black.
Claws: Dark horn color.
Eyes: Dark brown.

Blue: See color photo on page 48.
Coat color: A strong, rich medium to dark blue, which extends over the entire body evenly. The under color is the same but a shade lighter. Whiskers blue.
Claws: Horn color.
Eyes: Blue.

Squirrel Gray: See color photo on page 10.
Coat color: The cover coat of the entire body is an even bluish gray, which may be lighter or darker. The under color is also bluish gray, and the intermediate band of the hairs is a light brownish color. A variegated, pearllike look is created by the longer guard hairs, which have light and dark ticking at the tips. These hairs should be clearly visible. Whiskers black.
Claws: Horn color.
Eyes: Bluish gray.

Agouti or Wild (Gray): See color photo on page 48.

Coat color: The color of this variety is very similar to the coloration of wild rabbits. The intermediary color is brownish, and the under color, blue. The back has a sprinkling of longer, black-tipped guard hairs, which create an effect of dark shading. The cover color of the chest and sides is somewhat lighter, and a wedge-shaped patch on the nape of the neck is rust-brown. The belly, underside of tail, inside of legs, and the jowls are white (this pattern is typical for wild rabbits). Whiskers black.
Claws: Dark horn color.
Eyes: Brown.

A Thuringian dwarf doe with her two young.
Above left: The five-day-old young in their nest. Above right: This baby dwarf rabbit makes a nice handful at twenty days. Below: The mother with her two twenty-day-old offspring.

Dwarf Breeds and Color Varieties

Varieties of Markings

The varieties described in this section are not referred to by their colors but by their markings, because their distinctive look is due less to overall color than to the pattern of the markings.

"Rus," Himalayan, or Himpole Black-and-white

Coat color and markings: The ground color is snow white. Against this, a dark mask stands out that covers the nose but should not extend higher than the eyes. The Himalayan dwarf has black ears and black "boots." The standard prescribes that both the front and the back legs, as well as the tail, be dark. The markings are most perfect in the winter. In such a situation we speak of "cold-induced" coloring. In the cold season the ground color is a pure snow white, and the markings are dark brown to black. In the summer, the white fur often gets a yellowish or darkish tinge, and the markings grow paler. The fur of the young is pure white all over; the markings don't begin to show up until around eight weeks. Whiskers black.

"Rus" or Himalayan Blue-and-white: The same as the "Rus" Black-and-white, except that the markings are blue.

Claws: Dark brown.
Eyes: Albino eyes; that is, no color pigment. They look red to pinkish red.

Thuringian: See color photos on back cover and on page 47.

Coat color and markings: Thuringian dwarfs

Prize-winning dwarf rabbits.
Above left: Gray dwarf (buck). Above right: Red dwarf (doe). Center left: Brown Marten dwarf (doe). Center right: Blue dwarf (doe). Below left: Lop-eared dwarf, bicolored gray-and-white (buck). Below right: Black dwarf (buck).

have dark masks, but these are less sharply delineated than in the "Rus" variety. On the back and sides there are patches of gray like a dusting of soot. The base color is not a pure yellow but more a reddish tan. The young are generally quite light, with the dark coloration appearing only later. The darkest markings—on the ears, nose, and legs—are particularly late in showing up (see color photo on page 47; here the markings are already visible in the nest young). Whiskers dark brown-black. This variety is rather popular in Europe but not often seen elsewhere.

Claws: Dark horn color.
Eyes: Brown.

White-tipped (Black): See color photos on back cover and on pages 9, 10, and 27.

Coat color: The ground color is pure black. (In White-tipped Blues the ground color is blue.) Standing out sharply against this dark background is the white on the belly, the inside of the legs, the underside of the tail, the eye rings, the nostrils, and the jowls. A wedge-shaped area on the nape is silvery gray to white. The white-tipped guard hairs, which are lacking in Black-and-tan and Brown-and-tan dwarfs, are clearly apparent. They extend up from the white underside and should be as evenly distributed as possible. Whiskers black.

Claws: Dark.
Eyes: Dark brown (bluish gray in White-tipped Blues).

Marten (Brown, Blue, and Yellow or Siamese): See color photos on inside front cover and on pages 10, 28, and 37 (Siamese) and on page 48 (Brown).

Coat color: The ground colors are light brown (Brown), light blue (Blue), and cream (Yellow, also called Siamese) The markings consist of a dark mask, dark ears, legs, and tail, a dark stripe down the back, and some darkening on the haunches and the shoulders. This last feature has been bred into the Brown Marten with particular success. Whiskers brown.

Claws: Dark (horn colored in Siamese).

Eyes: Dark brown (bluish gray in Brown Martens).

New Breeds Not Yet Officially Recognized

Japanese See color photo on page 28.

Coat color and markings: It is extremely hard to breed dwarfs with Japanese markings. Ideally the ground color is a rich yellow. On both flanks there are black stripes that ought to be as sharply delineated from the yellow ground color as possible. There should be at least four distinct black patches on each side. The most highly prized Japanese dwarfs are asymmetrically marked; for example, left side of head yellow with black ear, right front leg black and left one yellow. (The ears can also be marbled.)

Claws: Dark (light horn if the toes are yellow or marbled).

Eyes: Brown.

Brown-and-tan, Black-and-tan: See color photos on back cover and on page 9.

Coat color and markings: The tan color is the same in both varieties. The contrasting color should be clearly set off from it. This creates a strikingly handsome effect, particularly in the Black-and-tan variety. Nostrils, jowls, eye rings, rims of ears, and insides of legs are tan, as are the chest, belly, and a wedge-shaped patch on the nape. The darker color, which extends evenly over the upper part of the body, is a glossy black or dark brown. Whiskers black.

Claws: Dark to blackish brown.

Eyes: Brown.

Lop-eared Dwarfs

See color photos on back cover, inside back cover, and on pages 10 and 48.

Weight: These dwarf rabbits are somewhat heavier than the other dwarf varieties. Lop-eared dwarfs may weigh up to 3 lb. 14 oz. (1.75 kg)—the top weight for Polish rabbits and normal color dwarf rabbits is 2.2 pounds (1 kg).

Body type: Short and blocky body with wide, rounded hindquarters; neck strong without visible narrowing between head and body; well-developed jowls, broad forehead, and a ram's nose.

Ears: There are ridges or welts at the base of the ears, and the ears themselves look somewhat like ram's ears. They droop down with the inside of the ear against the head, forming a kind of horseshoe shape. In keeping with the animal's dwarf status, the lop-eared dwarf rabbit's ears are comparatively short, namely 9 to ll inches (22–28 cm). Normal-sized (5 kg) French lop-eared rabbits have ears 15 to l8 inches long (38–45 cm).

Coat: Dense and soft. Colors as in normal dwarf varieties. Agouti, however, is the most common color in the dwarf lops.

Claws and Eyes: Appropriate to the coat color.

Understanding Dwarf Rabbits

Rabbits and Hares

Rabbits and hares look alike in many cases and belong to the same family, the Leporidae. There is some confusion when vernacular terms are used, however. We speak, for example, of the jackrabbit, although it is really a hare. The main difference between rabbits and hares is that baby rabbits are naked, blind, and helpless at birth, while newborn hares are well-furred and can hop around soon after they are born. Hares cannot be domesticated, and they do not mate with rabbits, whether domestic or wild. Although some domestic rabbits resemble hares, with their slender form and long legs, they simply represent one of the many ways in which man has modified the Old World rabbit (*Oryctolagus cuniculus*). Hence the Belgian Hare—at one time the most popular breed in the U.K. and the United States— is a rabbit and cannot be successfully crossed with a wild hare.

Neither hares nor rabbits are rodents, although both love to chew. As already mentioned, they belong to the family Leporidae. In 1912, after considerable scientific debate, this family was removed from the order Rodentia and assigned to a separate mammalian order, Lagomorpha, on the basis of differences in movement and in the structure and function of the teeth.

From Wild Rabbit to Dwarf Rabbit

Did you know that Spain owes its Latin name Hispania to wild rabbits? Actually, the name arose from a minor mistake on the part of the Phoenicians who landed on the Iberian Peninsula around 1100 B.C. and found innumerable wild rabbits there. The sailors did not know rabbits, but they were familiar with a small, agouti-colored creature, the hyrax, which resembles the Peruvian guinea pig in shape and size and has similar hooves. The rabbits darting around among the rocks no doubt reminded the Phoenicians of the hyrax, and so the sailors named the peninsula *i-shepan-im*, which means "island of the hyrax," which later turned into Hispania. After this first mark in history, the existence of rabbits is well recorded. The Romans kept rabbits in large outdoor runs. During the Middle Ages, monks "bred" them in monasteries, particularly in France. And from there, the first domesticated rabbits

Wild rabbits (left) and hares (right) differ not only in their way of life but also—as you can see here—in their build.

came to England and Scandinavia. Various fancy rabbit breeds have been exhibited at shows since the early nineteenth century. It was not until the early 1970s that the miniatures of the rabbit fancy, the Netherland Dwarfs, were seen on American shores.

Initially, the production of meat and fur was the primary reason for domesticating rabbits. But soon an ambition to develop certain traits and an appreciation of different this way with each other when they feel varieties and colors developed, which led to deliberate selective breeding and to exhibitions. In this process, the ordinary domestic rabbit gradually changed into a purebred creature. It is not surprising that even before the turn of the century a new class of rabbits made its appearance, namely, the dwarf rabbits, which were shown at Hull in England about 1884.

Breeders in Germany, England, and especially Holland tried to breed dwarfs from white Polish rabbits. But it took until about 1940 before the Dutchman J. Hoefman, from Den Briel, succeeded in crossing a Ruby-eyed White with a wild rabbit. Holland is also the country that later (1949) supplied England and the rest of Europe with the first colored dwarf varieties. At first these rabbits weighed up to 4.4 pounds (2 kg), but gradually they became smaller and lighter and acquired today's typical dwarf look with the round, broad head and short ears.

The Behavior of Rabbits

Somewhere among the ancestors of every dwarf rabbit there is a Polish white and a wild rabbit. And no matter how unusual and colorful its fur, how short its ears, how weak its heart, its behavior is the same as that of these distant ancestors. This is true whether the rabbit lives in an outdoor hutch or has the run of your apartment. If you want to understand your little friend better, learn about his natural behavior patterns and know what his body movements and the sounds he produces mean.

Rabbits are almost entirely silent. In nature they have a great many enemies, and they lack weapons for defense. Wild rabbits cannot afford to hop around the countryside barking, grunting, bellowing, or yowling. Wild rabbits communicate among themselves by sniffing and by body language. We humans, too, once had more differentiated noses, as expressions like "having a good nose" attest to. And we, too, have a body language, although nowadays we mostly use it in a subconscious or unconscious way.

Body Language

Standing upright (see color photo on page 37): This posture allows the rabbit to get a better view of its surroundings, for instance as in tall grass. Rabbits also rise up on their hind feet to reach food they like (twigs and branches). When a rabbit jumps up in the cage and stands on its hind feet when you approach, this is a greeting and expresses anticipatory pleasure at being let out or fed.

Rolling: This is a sign of well-being. Your dwarf rabbit will have a tendency to roll in the peat or sand of the litter box.

Relaxed squatting with ears folded back: This is a resting posture. Try not to disturb the animal at these times.

Relaxed squatting with apparent chewing motions: Rabbits like to sit peacefully, moving their jaws.

Lying on one side with a leg stretched out and the eyes beginning to close (see drawing on page 20): The rabbit is going to sleep.

Nudging with the nose: Sometimes this is simply a gesture of greeting, but it is also meant to encourage petting.

Forceful pushing away of the hand: This signals that the rabbit has had enough.

Licking of the hand: This means Thank-you in rabbit language. Wild rabbits express their liking for each other by mutual licking.

Rubbing up against things with the chin: The rabbit is leaving its mark on the objects with the help of a scent-producing gland located under the chin. (The smell is imperceptible for humans.) The scent markings serve as identifying signs and claims of ownership.

Ingesting fecal matter: Certain feces are usually eaten just after they have been produced. They are excretions from the cecum and are not round and dry like normal rabbit feces but moist, glistening, and kidney-shaped (see drawing on page 16). They are an important source of vitamin B.

Tense stance with tail pointing straight up and head stretched forward: This posture indicates concentration, nervousness, and heightened curiosity. If the rabbit also folds its ears down (see drawing on page 14), this is a sign of defensiveness. An attack may follow any moment.

Stamping and drumming with the hind feet: This can be an expression of fear or a threatening or warning gesture. (Wild rabbits drum loudly with their feet at the approach

At a sign of sudden danger, dwarf rabbits flatten themselves against the ground with ears folded back.

of an enemy to warn their fellows and send them running for their burrows.)

Scratching and digging in the apartment: This behavior grows out of the rabbit's natural digging instinct. Sometimes it signals a need for attention.

Lying flat on the floor with ears folded back (see drawing below): The rabbit is trying to become invisible. This is a reaction to sudden danger and unexpected, loud noises. (The next step may be panicked flight. Watch out. The animal might hurt itself in a wild dash.)

Sound Utterances

The sounds of dwarf rabbits, like those of their wild cousins, are almost always very soft and far from assertive. You have to listen very carefully or you won't hear them at all.

Spitting: This is a brief spitting sound and may signal imminent attack; it always is an expression of aggression.

Brief growling: This sound is produced mostly by males shortly after mating.

Soft squeaking: Baby rabbits sometimes squeak when they are afraid or hungry (or, occasionally, when they are taken from the nest).

Grinding teeth: Violent grinding of the teeth, combined with a dull, staring look in the eyes, is always a sign that the animal is in great pain (as from tympanites). It should not be confused with the silent chewing motions of contentment.

Piercing, high-pitched cry: This cry is emitted only by an animal in mortal terror or in horrible pain.

Soft noise of teeth rubbing together: If you scratch your rabbit behind the ears, it will move its jaws in enjoyment. (Not all rabbits do this.)

completely secure and at ease. Mother rabbits often coo when nursing their young. The sound can be quite varied and is reminiscent of the cooing of doves, but the cooing of rabbits is less even and deeper in pitch.

Sensory Capacities

Rabbits can see better than hares, and they also hear very well. But their most acute sense organ is the nose, which is always in motion, sometimes wrinkling up or twisting sideways almost grotesquely. Not even the faintest scent escapes its notice. Wild rabbits—and our tame dwarf rabbits as well—leave scent marks wherever they go. An anal gland imparts a scent to the droppings, which to us humans have a sweetish smell; and with the aid of a scent gland under the chin, entries and exits of the burrow, clumps of grass, or posts are marked. In an apartment, chair and table legs, the cage, food dish, and sleeping house are similarly treated. The nose also plays a role in communication. Around the central burrow of one family of wild rabbits, English scientists found some thirty defecation spots—smelly border markers—that delineated the clan's territory. The animals responded with extreme agitation when a strange pile of droppings was deliberately placed near their burrow.

Bucks spray their chosen mates with urine to express affection and ownership at the same time. When two wild rabbits meet, they first sniff each other at length (the so-called contact sniffing).

A wild rabbit has to be able to find its way home in a hurry when danger appears (pursuit by an enemy). That is why all the habitual paths to feeding places and back to the burrow are clearly marked. Tame dwarf rabbits make use of the same system and thus find their way around your apartment, the balcony, or the garden quite easily. In a completely new environment that is not yet marked, as on an outing, a dwarf rabbit will proceed with extreme caution. It will keep rising up on its hind legs, moving its ears in all directions like a TV antenna, and looking and sniffing all around. It will also keep hopping back to you because you are its place of refuge. If there is an unexpected noise, the rabbit will take flight or flatten itself against the ground with ears down. Everything new is first and foremost a fear-inspiring shock, and it takes some time before the rabbit is convinced that there are no grounds for worry.

In a family of wild rabbits even the youngest members have already learned how important the sense of smell is for survival. The doe builds her nest burrow at some distance from the central burrow. She prepares the nest with a soft and warm lining of wool plucked from her belly, and the entry is covered with dirt and marked. Once the young are born, the doe slips into the nest once a day to nurse them (according to observations made by scientists). Guided only by their sense of smell, the baby rabbits—naked, blind, and deaf at first—nevertheless manage to find their mother's teats within seconds. They then proceed to consume milk—as much as 25% of their body weight within two minutes. Then the mother leaves and covers up the entrance again in a hurry, so that enemies won't get a chance to discover her nest. The young remain alone. If the mother spends a moment too long in the nest burrow, which has only one hole for entry and exit, this could spell doom—martens, foxes, and weasels are always on the lookout.

Useful Addresses

The American Rabbit Breeders Association (A.R.B.A.)
1925B South Main
Bloomington, Illinois 61701, U.S.A.

The A.R.B.A. publishs a magazine devoted to the fancy: *Domestic Rabbits*. It contains much useful information on breeds old and new, supplies of stock and equipment, as well as news of the shows that are held regularly in most parts of the country. The annual subscription is small, and there are reduced fees for children, pensioners, and family groups.

Another interesting monthly magazine is *Rabbits*
Countryside Publications, Ltd.
312 Portland Road, Highway 19 East
Waterloo, Wisconsin 53594, U.S.A.

The fanciers of Netherland Dwarf Rabbits have their own organization. For additional information, contact the following

American Netherland Dwarf Rabbit Club
Donna Decker, Secretary-Treasurer
P. O. Box 99
Mustang, Oklahoma 93064, U.S.A.

All serious rabbit fanciers in the U.K. should subscribe to the fortnightly magazine *Fur and Feather,* the official magazine of the British Rabbit Council (B.R.C.).

British Rabbit Council
Purfoy House
7 Kirkgate
Newark
Nottingham, England

Membership in the B.R.C. is also essential for the English rabbit enthusiast, as this is the governing body of the fancy. The annual subscription is small, and there are reduced fees for children, family groups, pensioners, etc. There are official series of rabbit rings supplied by the Council to members, the use of which helps to maintain records of the stock held by thousands of fanciers.

Index